DR. AMELIA HARTLEY. PH.D.

The protagonists mission:

To my dearest mom,

This book, The Protagonists' Mission, is dedicated to you, the guiding light in my life. From the moment I took my first breath, you have been there, nurturing, supporting, and encouraging me every step of the way. Your unwavering love and belief in me have been the foundation upon which I have built my dreams.

Contents

1.

2.

3.

4.

5.

6.

7.

8.

9.

10.

11.

12.

13.

14.

15.

16.

17.

18.

19.

20.

21.

22.

23.

Foreword

In the realm of literature, we embark on countless journeys alongside characters who strive to fulfill their destinies, overcome adversities, and ultimately leave an indelible mark on our hearts and minds. The Protagonists' Mission is no exception. Within its pages lies a tale that will transport readers to a world teeming with mystery, intrigue, and the unyielding pursuit of truth.

At its core, this book is a testament to the power of human resilience, unity, and the unwavering belief in the possibility of change. The protagonists, each with their unique strengths and vulnerabilities, are thrust into an extraordinary mission that will test their mettle, challenge their convictions, and force them to confront the darkest corners of their existence.

As we begin this narrative, we are introduced to a society on the brink of collapse. A world shrouded in secrecy, where the forces of oppression and manipulation have taken hold. The protagonists, ordinary individuals thrust into extraordinary circumstances, find themselves at the forefront of a rebellion against an oppressive regime that has long held sway over their lives.

The mission that lies before them is multifaceted, with layers upon layers of complexity. It is a quest that will require not only physical prowess but also emotional resilience, intellectual acumen, and deep-rooted empathy. With each step they take, the protagonists uncover a web of deceit, unearthing long-buried secrets that threaten to unravel the very fabric of their society.

But this is not merely a story of conflict and strife. It is a tale that delves into the intricacies of human relationships, the intricate dance between love and betrayal, and the unbreakable bonds forged in the crucible of adversity. As the protagonists navigate the treacherous path laid before them, they discover allies in unexpected places and courage within themselves that they never knew existed.

Throughout their journey, the protagonists will encounter a myriad of challenges that will test their resolve and push them to their limits. From heart-stopping encounters with the forces of darkness to soul-searching moments of introspection, each trial serves as a crucible in which the protagonists are forged into something greater than themselves.

In this book, readers will be transported to a world both familiar and fantastical, where the line between reality and myth blurs and the true nature of heroism is unveiled. It is a world of hidden wonders, where ancient prophecies and forgotten truths intertwine, and where the fate of an entire civilization hangs in the balance.

As we embark on this journey together, let us remember that within the pages of this book lies not only an escape from reality but also a mirror reflecting the triumphs and tribulations of our own lives. The

Protagonists' Mission invites us to question our own beliefs, challenge the status quo, and dare to dream of a better world.

So, dear reader, join me as we delve into this extraordinary tale of courage, sacrifice, and the unyielding power of the human spirit. Let us embark on a mission that will forever change the way we perceive our own lives and the world in which we inhabit.

May this book be a beacon of hope, inspiration, and a reminder that even in the face of insurmountable odds, we possess the ability to reshape our destinies and create a brighter future?

Safe travels,

[Dr. Amelia Hartley. PhD.]

Acknowledgement

Writing a book is a journey that is rarely undertaken alone. It is a collaborative effort that requires the support, guidance, and inspiration of numerous individuals who contribute their time, expertise, and unwavering belief in the power of storytelling. As I reflect upon the completion of The Protagonists' Mission, I am overwhelmed with gratitude for all those who have played a part in bringing this story to life.

First and foremost, I would like to express my deepest appreciation to my family and friends. Your unwavering support, encouragement, and understanding have been the foundation upon which this book was built. Your belief in me and my abilities has been a constant source of motivation, and I am forever grateful for your presence in my life.

To my editor, whose keen insights and expert guidance have helped shape this story into its final form, I extend my utmost gratitude. Your commitment to the craft of storytelling and your dedication to helping me refine my words have been invaluable. Your belief in the potential of this story has pushed me to strive for excellence, and I am deeply grateful for your unwavering support.

I would also like to extend my gratitude to the team at the publishing house who have worked tirelessly to bring this book to fruition.

From the cover design to the marketing efforts, your passion and expertise have been instrumental in ensuring that The Protagonists' Mission reaches the hands of readers around the world. Your commitment to the written word is commendable, and I am honored to have had the opportunity to work with you.

To the beta readers and early reviewers who provided invaluable feedback and constructive criticism, thank you. Your insights and perspectives have helped shape this story, making it stronger, more cohesive, and more engaging. Your dedication to the craft of storytelling and your willingness to invest your time and energy in the development of this book is deeply appreciated.

I would also like to express my gratitude to the countless authors whose works have inspired me and shaped my writing journey. Your words have served as guiding lights, illuminating the path before me and reminding me of the power and beauty of storytelling. It is through your works that I have learned the art of crafting compelling characters, building immersive worlds, and weaving intricate narratives. I am forever indebted to you for sharing your wisdom and creativity.

To the readers who have embarked on this journey with me, thank you. It is your curiosity, your open mind, and your willingness to explore new worlds that breathe life into these pages. Your support and engagement are what makes the act of writing truly meaningful. I hope that The Protagonists' Mission has brought you joy, inspiration, and a renewed sense of the power of storytelling.

Lastly, I would like to express my deepest gratitude to the characters themselves. Although born from my imagination, they have taken on lives of their own, becoming friends, confidants, and sources of inspiration. They have taught me the importance of resilience, compassion, and the unwavering pursuit of truth. It is through their struggles, triumphs, and growth that The Protagonists' Mission has come to life. I am humbled and honored to have been entrusted with their stories.

In conclusion, writing The Protagonists' Mission has been a transformative experience, one that would not have been possible without the support and contributions of a remarkable community of individuals. To every person who has played a part in this journey, whether directly or indirectly, I extend my deepest gratitude. Your belief in the power of storytelling, your unwavering support, and your presence in my life have been the driving forces behind this book. Thank you for joining me on this adventure, and may the stories we tell continue to inspire, empower, and shape the world we live in.

With heartfelt appreciation,

[Dr. Amelia Hartley. PhD.]

Description

"The Protagonist Mission" is an exhilarating and thought-provoking science fiction novel that takes readers on an extraordinary journey through time, space, and the complexities of human existence. Set in a future world where advanced technology intertwines with ethical dilemmas, this gripping tale explores the boundless potential of the human spirit and the power of determination.

In a society dominated by a powerful conglomerate known as the Global Nexus Corporation, we meet our protagonist, a young and brilliant scientist named Dr. Amelia Hartley. Driven by a deep sense of curiosity and a desire to unravel the mysteries of the universe, Amelia finds herself embarking on an unprecedented mission that will challenge everything she knows and believes.

Amelia's mission begins when she discovers a hidden message within a seemingly innocuous scientific research paper. The message, encoded with cryptic symbols, leads her to uncover a secret society known as The Protagonists. Dedicated to preserving the balance between technology and humanity, this clandestine organization reveals to Amelia a startling truth: the fabric of reality itself is at stake.

As Amelia delves deeper into the world of The Protagonists, she learns of their ancient origins and their ongoing struggle against the oppressive forces of the Global Nexus Corporation. With each revelation, Amelia finds herself entangled in a web of political conspiracies, personal sacrifices, and moral dilemmas. Alongside a diverse group of allies, she must navigate treacherous landscapes, both physical and ideological, to confront the Corporation's tyrannical grip on society.

"The Protagonist Mission" combines elements of hard science fiction, suspenseful espionage, and philosophical exploration. The narrative seamlessly weaves together complex scientific concepts with intricate character development, allowing readers to immerse themselves in a world where technology and humanity collide. As Amelia races against time to fulfill her mission, she grapples with questions of identity, free will, and the nature of progress itself.

Through vivid descriptions and evocative prose, the author transports readers to vividly imagined locations, from sprawling futuristic cities to remote, untamed wilderness. The novel's pacing keeps readers on the edge of their seats, as each chapter unfolds with unexpected twists and turns. The story's rich tapestry of emotions, from heart-pounding action to introspective moments of introspection, ensures a deeply engaging reading experience.

"The Protagonist Mission" challenges readers to contemplate the implications of our ever-evolving relationship with technology. It invites us to reflect on the potential consequences of unchecked power, the importance of personal agency, and the capacity for hope in the face of seemingly insurmountable odds. This compelling narrative serves as a cautionary tale, reminding us of the fragile balance between progress and our shared humanity.

With its compelling characters, intricate plot, and thought-provoking themes, "The Protagonist Mission" is a must-read for science fiction enthusiasts, fans of dystopian literature, and anyone who appreciates a gripping tale that explores the depths of human potential. Prepare to embark on a thrilling adventure that will challenge your perceptions and leave you questioning the very nature of reality itself.

Part One

Life is a beautiful, yet complex journey that we embark upon with the hope of finding purpose and fulfillment. We all strive to create a meaningful life, one that is rich with experiences, relationships, and personal growth. But how can we truly achieve this? In this part, we will explore some key principles and practices that can guide us toward creating a life filled with meaning.

Creating a Meaningful Life.

Life is a beautiful, yet complex journey that we embark upon with the hope of finding purpose and fulfillment. We all strive to create a meaningful life, one that is rich with experiences, relationships, and personal growth. But how can we truly achieve this? In this part, we will explore some key principles and practices that can guide us toward creating a life filled with meaning.

First and foremost, it is essential to define what a meaningful life means to us as individuals. This introspection allows us to identify our core values, passions, and aspirations. By understanding what truly matters to us, we can align our actions and choices accordingly. A meaningful life is not a one-size-fits-all concept; it is deeply personal and unique to each person.

One crucial aspect of cultivating a meaningful life is pursuing our passions and interests. Engaging in activities that bring us joy and fulfillment can significantly enhance our overall well-being. Whether it's painting, playing an instrument, writing, or engaging in sports, dedicating time to our passions allows us to express ourselves authentically and connect with our inner selves.

Meaningful connections and relationships form another vital ingredient in the recipe for a meaningful life. Humans are social beings, and fostering positive and supportive relationships with family, friends, and the community can bring immense joy and fulfillment. Actively listening, showing empathy, and investing time and effort into nurturing these connections can create a sense of belonging and purpose.

Contributing to something greater than ourselves is another powerful way to infuse meaning into our lives. Engaging in acts of service, volunteering, or participating in community initiatives can have a profound impact not only on those we help but also on our sense of purpose. By making a positive difference in the lives of others, we find a deeper meaning and a sense of fulfillment that transcends personal achievements.

Self-reflection and personal growth are integral components of a meaningful life. Taking the time to evaluate our thoughts, emotions, and actions allows us to gain self-awareness and make positive changes. Setting meaningful goals and continuously striving to learn and grow challenges us to reach our full potential and discover new aspects of ourselves.

Living in the present moment is a fundamental principle of creating a meaningful life. Often, we get caught up in worrying about the future or dwelling on the past, forgetting to appreciate the beauty and opportunities that the present holds. By cultivating mindfulness and practicing gratitude, we can savor the simple pleasures, find joy in everyday moments, and create a deeper sense of fulfillment.

Chapter 1: The Four Roles We Play in Life.

The Victim, the Villain, the Protagonist, and the Guide.

In the grand tapestry of life, we all assume various roles that shape our experiences and interactions. These roles, often intertwined and ever-changing, encompass the breadth of human existence. In this chapter, we explore the four archetypal roles we play in life: the victim, the villain, the protagonist, and the guide. These roles serve as lenses through which we perceive and engage with the world, influencing our thoughts, actions, and relationships. By understanding and embracing these roles, we can gain insight into our journeys and cultivate empathy for others. This chapter delves into each role, highlighting their characteristics, significance, and impact on personal growth and societal dynamics.

1. The Victim.

The victim is a role that many of us assume at various points in our lives. Victims tend to perceive themselves as powerless and subject to the circumstances they find themselves in. They often feel victimized by external forces, blaming others or fate for their misfortunes. This role can be both limiting and disempowering, preventing individuals from taking responsibility for their lives and hindering personal growth. However, understanding the victim archetype allows us to empathize with those who have experienced genuine hardships and trauma. It reminds us of the importance of compassion and support for those in need.

2. The Villain.

The villain is a role often demonized, yet it is an integral part of the human experience. Villains are characterized by their negative actions, harmful intentions, or disruptive behavior. They are often seen as antagonists, causing suffering and chaos in the lives of others. However, beneath the surface, villains may be driven by their pain, fear, or insecurities. Recognizing the villain within ourselves enables us to confront and transform our negative tendencies. Furthermore, understanding the motivations and struggles of villains fosters empathy and forgiveness, leading to healing and reconciliation.

3. The Protagonist.

The protagonist is the role that embodies the hero, the central character in our narratives. Protagonists are driven by goals, dreams, and aspirations, and they actively strive to overcome obstacles in their quest for success and fulfillment. They inspire us to embrace courage, resilience, and determination. By assuming the role of the protagonist in our own lives, we take ownership of our actions, make choices aligned with our values, and create our desired outcomes.

The protagonist's role empowers us to shape our destiny, learn from failures, and celebrate victories.

4. The Guide.

The guide role encompasses mentors, teachers, and all those who provide guidance, wisdom, and support to others. Guides possess knowledge, experience, and insight that help individuals navigate challenges, discover their strengths, and unlock their potential. They serve as beacons of inspiration, offering guidance and encouragement along the journey. Assuming the guide role allows us to make a positive impact on the lives of others, fostering growth, and transformation. It reinforces the importance of mentorship, community, and interconnectedness in our collective human experience.

Tips for Navigating the Four Roles in Life.

1. **Self-Reflection:** Take time for introspection and self-reflection to understand which role you tend to embody in different situations. Recognizing patterns and tendencies will allow you to navigate these roles more consciously and make intentional choices.

2. **Cultivate Empathy:** Develop empathy by putting yourself in the shoes of others who may be playing different roles. This helps you understand their perspectives, challenges, and motivations, fostering compassion and promoting healthier relationships.

3. **Embrace Responsibility:** Embrace responsibility for your actions and choices. Rather than playing the victim, take ownership of your circumstances and seek ways to create positive change. Empower yourself to be the protagonist of your own life story.

4. **Practice Forgiveness:** In situations where you perceive someone as a villain, practice forgiveness. Understand that people's actions are often influenced by their struggles and insecurities. Forgiveness frees you from carrying the burden of resentment and promotes personal healing.

5. **Seek Guidance:** Embrace the guide role by seeking guidance from mentors, teachers, or role models. Their wisdom and support can provide valuable insights and help you navigate challenges more effectively. Additionally, be open to becoming a guide for others, sharing your experiences and knowledge to uplift and inspire.

Benefits of Understanding and Embracing the Four Roles.

1. **Personal Growth:** Recognizing and embracing these roles enables personal growth by promoting self-awareness, introspection, and self-reflection. It allows you to break free from limiting patterns and develop a deeper understanding of yourself.

2. **Empathy and Compassion:** Understanding the four roles cultivates empathy and compassion. It reminds us that everyone experiences different perspectives and struggles,

fostering a greater sense of understanding and connection with others.

3. **Resilience and Empowerment:** Embracing the protagonist's role empowers you to take control of your life, make conscious choices, and overcome obstacles. It instills resilience, as you learn from failures, adapt, and strive for personal fulfillment.

4. **Healing and Reconciliation:** Recognizing the villain role within ourselves promotes healing and reconciliation. By understanding our negative tendencies and those of others, we can work towards forgiveness, reconciliation, and building healthier relationships.

5. **Positive Impact on Others:** Embracing the guide role allows you to make a positive impact on the lives of others. By sharing your knowledge, experiences, and wisdom, you can guide and inspire others on their journeys of personal growth and transformation.

Functions of the Four Roles.

1. **Self-Reflection and Awareness:** The four roles serve as tools for self-reflection and self-awareness, helping us understand our thoughts, emotions, and behaviors in different situations.

2. **Understanding Human Behavior:** These roles provide insights into the complexities of human behavior, shedding light on the motivations, struggles, and dynamics that influence our interactions with others.

3. **Relationship Dynamics:** The roles influence how we relate to others and shape our relationships. Understanding these roles can help us navigate conflicts, cultivate empathy, and build healthier connections.

4. **Personal Agency and Empowerment:** Embracing the protagonist role empowers individuals to take agency over their lives, make conscious choices, and actively shape their narratives.

5. **Social Dynamics and Collective Well-being:** These roles contribute to the broader social fabric. By recognizing and embracing the guide role, individuals can positively impact others and contribute to the collective well-being of society.

Techniques for Navigating the Four Roles in Life.

1. **Self-Awareness:** Cultivate self-awareness by practicing mindfulness and introspection. This allows you to observe your thoughts, emotions, and behaviors, helping you recognize when you are embodying a particular role and enabling you to make conscious choices.

2. **Emotional Regulation:** Develop techniques for emotional regulation, such as deep breathing exercises, journaling, or seeking support from trusted individuals. This helps you navigate challenging situations and prevents you from being overwhelmed by negative emotions associated with any of the roles.

3. **Cognitive Restructuring:** Engage in cognitive restructuring by challenging negative thought patterns and replacing them

with more positive and empowering beliefs. This technique
helps you reframe situations and shift your perspective,
allowing you to break free from victimhood or villainous
tendencies.

4. **Empathy Development:** Practice empathy by actively
   putting yourself in the shoes of others. This involves listening
   attentively, seeking to understand their experiences and
   perspectives, and suspending judgment. Developing empathy
   helps you relate to others in a more compassionate and
   understanding way.

5. **Goal Setting and Action Planning:** Embrace the role of the
   protagonist by setting meaningful goals and creating action
   plans to achieve them. Break down your goals into smaller,
   manageable steps, and take consistent action towards their
   realization. This technique empowers you to take charge of
   your life and create positive outcomes.

Factors Influencing the Four Roles.

1. **Personal History and Experiences:** Our past experiences,
   upbringing, and traumas can significantly influence the roles
   we assume in life. Difficult or traumatic experiences may
   lead individuals to embody the victim or villain role, while
   positive experiences can foster a more proactive and guiding
   mindset.

2. **Social Environment:** The influence of our social
   environment, including family, friends, and culture, plays a
   crucial role in shaping the roles we adopt. Social norms,

expectations, and interactions can impact our perception of ourselves and others.

3. **Belief Systems and Mindset:** Our beliefs and mindset shape our interpretation of events and determine the roles we take on. Limiting beliefs can reinforce victimhood or villainous tendencies while empowering beliefs can fuel the protagonist and guide roles.

4. **External Circumstances and Challenges:** External circumstances, such as socioeconomic factors, health issues, or life events, can contribute to the roles we play. Adversity may push individuals into the victim role, while power imbalances or injustice can trigger villainous behavior.

5. **Personal Agency and Choice:** Ultimately, the roles we play are influenced by our agency and the choices we make. It is within our power to consciously navigate and transform these roles, taking responsibility for our actions and embracing the roles that align with personal growth and well-being.

Causes for Assuming the Four Roles.

1. **Trauma and Victimization:** Experiencing trauma, abuse, or victimization can lead individuals to adopt the victim role as a means of coping with their pain and seeking support from others.

2. **Fear and Insecurity:** Fear and insecurity can drive individuals to embody the villain role, as they seek to exert control or protect themselves from perceived threats.

3. **Personal Ambitions and Aspirations:** The desire for personal growth, success, or recognition can motivate individuals to embody the protagonist role. They actively pursue their goals and overcome obstacles along the way.

4. **Mentorship and Guidance:** Receiving guidance and mentorship from others can inspire individuals to embrace the guide role. They share their knowledge and support others in their journeys.

5. **Societal Expectations and Pressures:** Societal expectations, cultural norms, and pressure to conform can influence the roles individuals assume. These external factors shape their behaviors and shape their interactions with others.

Importance of the Four Roles in Life.

1. **Self-Awareness:** Understanding the four roles allows for greater self-awareness, enabling individuals to recognize their patterns, tendencies, and behaviors in different life situations.

2. **Personal Growth:** Embracing and navigating these roles promotes personal growth by challenging individuals to confront their limitations, develop resilience, and strive for self-improvement.

3. **Empathy and Compassion:** Recognizing and embodying these roles fosters empathy and compassion, as individuals gain a deeper understanding of their struggles and those of others.

4. **Relationship Building:** The roles influence how individuals relate to others, allowing for healthier and more empathetic interactions, and fostering stronger and more fulfilling relationships.

5. **Emotional Intelligence:** Understanding these roles enhances emotional intelligence by enabling individuals to recognize and regulate their own emotions and empathize with the emotions of others.

6. **Conflict Resolution:** The awareness of these roles can facilitate conflict resolution by providing insight into the dynamics of different perspectives and promoting understanding and compromise.

7. **Personal Responsibility:** Recognizing these roles encourages individuals to take responsibility for their own lives, choices, and actions, empowering them to create positive change.

8. **Leadership Development:** Embracing the protagonist and guide roles nurtures leadership qualities, enabling individuals to inspire and guide others toward personal and collective growth.

9. **Resilience and Adaptability:** Navigating these roles develops resilience and adaptability, as individuals learn to navigate challenges, setbacks, and unexpected circumstances.

10. **Collective Well-being:** Understanding these roles contributes to the collective well-being of society by promoting empathy, compassion, and positive social dynamics.

Qualities Associated with the Four Roles.

1. **Victim:** Vulnerability, empathy, resilience, and the ability to seek support and healing.
2. **Villain:** Self-awareness, accountability, the capacity for self-reflection, and the potential for transformation.
3. **Protagonist:** Determination, courage, perseverance, self-belief, and the ability to inspire and motivate others.
4. **Guide:** Wisdom, empathy, patience, the ability to listen and provide guidance, and a desire to uplift and support others.

Framework for Understanding the Four Roles.

1. **Archetypal Psychology:** The four roles can be understood through the lens of archetypal psychology, exploring the collective unconscious and the universal patterns of human behavior.
2. **Narrative Therapy:** The roles can be explored within the framework of narrative therapy, examining the stories and narratives individuals create to make sense of their lives.
3. **Humanistic Psychology:** The roles reflect the humanistic psychology perspective, emphasizing personal growth, self-actualization, and the pursuit of individual potential.
4. **Social Constructivism:** The roles are shaped by social constructs and cultural influences, highlighting the role of society in shaping individual behavior and perceptions.

5. **Existentialism:** The roles can be examined through an existentialist lens, exploring the choices, responsibilities, and search for meaning in human existence.

6. **Cognitive-Behavioral Therapy:** The roles relate to cognitive-behavioral therapy, examining how thoughts, emotions, and behaviors influence individuals' experiences and interactions.

7. **Systems Theory:** The roles can be understood within the framework of systems theory, exploring how individuals' roles interact and influence the dynamics of relationships and social systems.

8. **Developmental Psychology:** The roles can be viewed through the lens of developmental psychology, examining how individuals progress and evolve in their roles across the lifespan.

9. **Transpersonal Psychology:** The roles relate to transpersonal psychology, exploring the spiritual and transcendent aspects of human existence beyond the individual ego.

10. **Positive Psychology:** The roles can be explored within the framework of positive psychology, focusing on personal strengths, resilience, and the pursuit of happiness and well-being.

Pros of the Four Roles in Life.

1. **Self-Awareness:** Recognizing the four roles allows individuals to develop a deeper understanding of their

behaviors, patterns, and motivations, leading to greater self-awareness.

2. **Personal Growth:** Embracing and navigating these roles promotes personal growth by challenging individuals to confront their limitations, develop resilience, and strive for self-improvement.

3. **Empathy and Compassion:** Understanding these roles fosters empathy and compassion, as individuals gain a deeper understanding of their struggles and those of others.

4. **Healthy Relationships:** Recognizing and embodying these roles promotes healthier and more empathetic interactions, leading to stronger and more fulfilling relationships.

5. **Personal Agency:** Understanding these roles empowers individuals to take responsibility for their lives, make conscious choices, and actively shape their narratives.

Cons of the Four Roles in Life.

1. **Limiting Beliefs:** Embodying the victim role can lead to the development of limiting beliefs, making it difficult to take responsibility for one's life and hindering personal growth.

2. **Negative Self-Perception:** Identifying with the villain role may lead to a negative self-perception, causing individuals to see themselves as inherently bad or unworthy.

3. **Conflict and Misunderstandings:** If individuals are unable to navigate these roles effectively, it can lead to conflicts, misunderstandings, and strained relationships with others.

4. **Stagnation:** Getting stuck in any one role, whether it's victimhood or villainy, can hinder personal growth and prevent individuals from reaching their full potential.
5. **Lack of Empathy:** Failing to understand and embody these roles can result in a lack of empathy and understanding towards oneself and others, leading to strained relationships and a lack of personal growth.

Chapter 2: Embracing Autonomy.

The Triumph of Protagonists.

Throughout literature and storytelling, protagonists often undergo transformative journeys that lead them to embrace their autonomy. This profound process of self-discovery and empowerment allows the protagonist to break free from societal constraints, challenge oppressive systems, and emerge as a beacon of individuality. By examining the experiences of protagonists who embrace their autonomy, we can understand the significance of this theme and its impact on personal growth and societal change.

1. Defying Societal Expectations.

In many narratives, protagonists find themselves trapped within the confines of societal expectations. They are burdened by the weight of conformity, leading to a sense of suffocation and unfulfillment. However, as the story unfolds, they gradually realize the importance of embracing their autonomy. Through acts of rebellion or self-reflection, they break free from the mold imposed upon them and embark on a journey of self-discovery.

2. Empowerment and Self-Realization.

The moment a protagonist embraces their autonomy marks a turning point in their narrative arc. It is a profound realization that they possess the power to shape their destiny. By acknowledging their true desires, strengths, and values, they become empowered to pursue their dreams. This newfound self-awareness allows them to break free from internal and external constraints, leading to personal growth and fulfillment.

3. Challenging Oppressive Systems.

Protagonists who embrace their autonomy often become catalysts for change within their respective societies. They challenge oppressive systems and ideologies, inspiring others to question and resist. Their autonomous actions may incite revolutions, spark social movements, or simply serve as an example of defiance against injustice. In doing so, they become agents of change and symbols of hope for a better world.

4. Overcoming Internal Struggles.

Embracing autonomy is not without its challenges. Protagonists often face internal struggles and self-doubt along their journey. It requires courage to reject societal norms and trust one's instincts. However, by overcoming these obstacles, the protagonist not only transforms themselves but also inspires others to overcome their internal battles, fostering a culture of self-acceptance and personal freedom.

Tips for Embracing Autonomy.

1. **Self-reflection:** Take time to reflect on your goals, values, and desires. Understand what truly matters to you and align your actions accordingly.

2. **Setting boundaries:** Establish clear boundaries to protect your time, energy, and resources. Learn to say no to things that don't align with your priorities and values.

3. **Decision-making:** Take ownership of your decisions and embrace the responsibility that comes with them. Trust yourself to make choices that align with your vision of success.

4. **Taking calculated risks:** Embrace the opportunity for growth by taking calculated risks. Step out of your comfort zone and explore new possibilities.

5. **Continuous learning:** Embrace a growth mindset and commit to lifelong learning. Seek new knowledge, acquire new skills, and adapt to changing circumstances.

Benefits of Embracing Autonomy.

1. **Personal fulfillment:** By embracing autonomy, you gain a sense of personal fulfillment as you align your actions with your values and pursue your path.

2. **Increased confidence:** Taking ownership of your decisions and actions boosts your confidence and self-esteem.

3. **Improved decision-making:** Autonomy allows you to make decisions based on your judgment and intuition, leading to better choices that align with your goals.

4. **Adaptability:** Autonomy fosters adaptability as you become more comfortable with change and better equipped to navigate evolving situations.

5. **Enhanced creativity:** Embracing autonomy encourages you to think outside the box, explore new ideas, and express your creativity freely.

Functions of Autonomy.

1. **Self-direction:** Autonomy enables you to direct your path and make choices independently, without excessive external influence.

2. **Empowerment:** Autonomy empowers you to take control of your life and make decisions that shape your future.

3. **Responsibility:** Autonomy encourages a sense of responsibility for your actions and their consequences.

4. **Individuality:** Autonomy allows you to express your unique identity and pursue your passions and interests.

5. **Growth and development:** Autonomy provides the space and freedom necessary for personal growth, self-discovery, and skill development.

Techniques for Embracing Autonomy.

1. **Mindfulness:** Practice being present and aware of your thoughts, feelings, and actions. Mindfulness helps you tune in to your inner voice and make conscious choices.

2. **Goal setting:** Set clear and meaningful goals that align with your values. Break them down into smaller, manageable steps to stay motivated and focused on your journey towards autonomy.

3. **Assertiveness:** Develop assertiveness skills to express your needs, opinions, and boundaries effectively. Communicate assertively to ensure your autonomy is respected by others.

4. **Self-care:** Prioritize self-care activities that nurture your physical, mental, and emotional well-being. Taking care of yourself enhances your ability to make autonomous decisions.

5. **Seeking support:** Surround yourself with a supportive network of friends, mentors, or professionals who can provide guidance, encouragement, and accountability on your path to autonomy.

Factors Influencing Autonomy.

1. **Personal beliefs and values:** Your individual beliefs and values shape your perspective on autonomy and influence your willingness to embrace it.

2. **Cultural and societal norms:** The cultural and societal context you are in can impact the level of autonomy you perceive as acceptable or desirable.

3. **Education and upbringing:** Your educational background and upbringing can influence your understanding of autonomy and how it should be exercised.

4. **External influences:** Various external factors such as family, friends, media, and social institutions can either support or hinder your autonomy.

5. **Self-awareness and self-confidence:** Your level of self-awareness and self-confidence play a role in your ability to recognize and assert your autonomy.

Causes of Embracing Autonomy.

1. **Desire for personal freedom:** The innate human desire for freedom and independence motivates individuals to embrace autonomy.

2. **Dissatisfaction with external control:** Feeling restricted or controlled by external forces can lead individuals to seek autonomy as a means of reclaiming their power.

3. **Need for self-expression:** Autonomy allows individuals to express their unique identities, values, and creativity freely.

4. **Personal growth and self-actualization:** Autonomy provides the space for personal growth, self-discovery, and the pursuit of one's aspirations.

5. **Empowerment and agency:** Embracing autonomy empowers individuals to take control of their lives, make decisions, and shape their destinies.

Importance of embracing autonomy and the triumph of the protagonist.

1. **Personal Growth:** Embracing autonomy allows individuals to take control of their lives and pursue personal growth. It enables them to explore their potential, develop new skills, and expand their horizons.

2. **Decision-making:** Autonomy empowers individuals to make their own decisions and take responsibility for the outcomes. It promotes critical thinking, problem-solving, and the ability to weigh options effectively.

3. **Self-Expression:** Autonomy grants individuals the freedom to express their thoughts, opinions, and creativity. It encourages authenticity and fosters a sense of individuality.

4. **Resilience:** Embracing autonomy helps individuals build resilience by developing the ability to adapt to change, overcome challenges, and bounce back from setbacks. It nurtures a sense of self-reliance and inner strength.

5. **Fulfillment and Satisfaction:** Autonomy allows individuals to align their actions with their values, passions, and goals. It can lead to a greater sense of fulfillment, satisfaction, and overall well-being.

Qualities of embracing autonomy and the triumph of the protagonist.

1. **Self-awareness:** Understanding one's strengths, weaknesses, and values is crucial for embracing autonomy. Self-

awareness enables individuals to make informed choices
aligned with their true selves.

2. **Confidence:** Having belief in oneself and one's abilities is a
key quality for embracing autonomy. Confidence empowers
individuals to take risks, step outside their comfort zone, and
pursue their aspirations.

3. **Initiative:** Taking initiative involves being proactive and
taking decisive action without waiting for others to lead. It
showcases a sense of ownership and a willingness to take
responsibility.

4. **Adaptability:** Embracing autonomy requires the ability to
adapt to changing circumstances and navigate through
uncertainty. Being flexible and open to new ideas and
perspectives is vital.

5. **Resilience:** Resilience allows individuals to bounce back
from setbacks, learn from failures, and persevere in the face
of adversity. It involves maintaining a positive mindset and
embracing challenges as opportunities for growth.

**The framework of embracing autonomy and the triumph of the
protagonist.**

A framework for embracing autonomy can include the following
elements:

1. **Goal Setting:** Clearly defining personal goals and objectives
provides a sense of direction and purpose.

2. **Self-reflection:** Regularly reflecting on one's values, strengths, and areas for improvement helps in making informed decisions.

3. **Decision-making:** Developing a systematic approach to decision-making, considering different perspectives and potential consequences, can enhance autonomy.

4. **Accountability:** Holding oneself accountable for actions and outcomes promotes a sense of ownership and self-responsibility.

5. **Continuous Learning:** Emphasizing ongoing learning and seeking new knowledge and skills is crucial for personal growth and autonomy.

Advantages of embracing autonomy and the triumph of the protagonist.

1. **Personal Freedom:** Embracing autonomy allows individuals to have control over their choices and actions, granting them the freedom to live life on their terms.

2. **Self-Discovery:** Autonomy provides an opportunity for individuals to explore their interests, values, and passions, leading to a deeper understanding of oneself and personal growth.

3. **Empowerment:** Embracing autonomy empowers individuals to take charge of their lives, make decisions that align with their values, and pursue their goals with confidence.

4. **Innovation and Creativity:** Autonomy encourages individuals to think outside the box, explore new ideas, and

express their creativity without being bound by external constraints.

5. **Resilience and Adaptability:** Embracing autonomy fosters resilience and adaptability as individuals learn to navigate challenges, overcome obstacles, and adapt to changing circumstances.

Disadvantages of embracing autonomy and the triumph of the protagonist.

1. **Increased Responsibility:** Embracing autonomy means taking on more responsibility for one's choices and actions, which can sometimes be overwhelming or burdensome.

2. **Lack of Guidance:** Without external guidance or structure, individuals embracing autonomy may face uncertainty or difficulty in decision-making, leading to confusion or indecisiveness.

3. **Potential Isolation:** Embracing autonomy may result in individuals feeling isolated or disconnected from others if they prioritize their independence over social connections.

4. **Fear of Failure:** When embracing autonomy, individuals may face a heightened fear of failure as they bear the consequences of their decisions alone.

5. **Overwhelming Choices:** With autonomy comes a multitude of choices, which can lead to decision fatigue or analysis paralysis if individuals struggle to prioritize or make decisions efficiently.

Chapter 3: Living a Meaningful Life.

T he Journey of the Protagonist.

In the vast tapestry of humani existence, the pursuit of a meaningful life stands as a universal aspiration. The protagonist, driven by a profound desire for purpose, embarks on a transformative journey to live a life of significance. This chapter will explores the protagonist's decision to embrace a meaningful life, delving into the various dimensions and challenges encountered along the way. Through introspection, self-discovery, and the pursuit of values, the protagonist's journey unfolds, illustrating the profound impact of choosing a life filled with purpose.

1. The Awakening: A Call for Meaning.

The protagonist's decision to live a meaningful life often stems from a profound awakening—an internal call that urges a departure from a mundane existence. It may be triggered by a significant life event, contemplation of mortality, or a realization of the fleeting nature of time. This awakening ignites a desire to seek deeper meaning beyond material pursuits, leading the protagonist on a transformative path.

2. The Quest for Purpose.

Having embraced the significance of a meaningful life, the protagonist embarks on a quest to discover their purpose. This quest involves introspection, self-reflection, and a deep exploration of personal values, passions, and talents. Through introspective practices such as meditation, journaling, and engaging in meaningful conversations, the protagonist begins to unravel their true essence and identify the activities and endeavors that align with their core values.

3. Aligning Actions with Values.

Living a meaningful life necessitates aligning one's actions with their values. The protagonist recognizes the importance of congruence between their beliefs and behaviors, striving to ensure that every decision and action reflects their authentic self. This alignment fosters a sense of integrity and wholeness, allowing the protagonist to navigate life with a deep sense of purpose and conviction.

4. Cultivating Meaningful Relationships.

As the protagonist continues their journey, they come to appreciate the significance of cultivating meaningful relationships. Meaningful connections with loved ones, friends, and community members contribute to a sense of belonging and purpose. The protagonist seeks to foster authentic and supportive relationships, nurturing a network of individuals who share their values and aspirations. These connections provide emotional support, collaboration, and opportunities for growth and fulfillment.

5. Impacting the World.

A meaningful life is not confined to personal fulfillment; it extends beyond the self to impact the world. The protagonist recognizes their capacity to make a positive difference in the lives of others and the wider society. Whether through acts of kindness, community service, or pursuing a career dedicated to a noble cause, the protagonist strives to leave a lasting impact on the world, contributing to the greater good and leaving a meaningful legacy.

6. Overcoming Challenges.

The protagonist's journey towards a meaningful life is not without challenges. They encounter obstacles such as self-doubt, societal pressures, and the fear of failure. However, these challenges become opportunities for growth and resilience. The protagonist develops inner strength, perseverance, and a mindset that embraces setbacks as valuable learning experiences. Through these trials, the protagonist becomes a testament to the power of determination and resilience in the pursuit of a meaningful life.

7. Embracing Transcendence.

In the pursuit of a meaningful life, the protagonist reaches a stage of transcendence—a state where personal growth and selflessness converge. The protagonist's focus shifts from personal fulfillment to contributing to something greater than themselves. This transcendence allows the protagonist to experience profound joy, fulfillment, and a deep connection with the world around them.

Tips for Living a Meaningful Life.

1. **Self-Reflection:** Take time for introspection and self-reflection to gain clarity about your values, passions, and aspirations. This self-awareness will guide you in making choices that align with your authentic self.

2. **Set Meaningful Goals:** Define meaningful goals that are in line with your values and purpose. These goals will provide direction and a sense of fulfillment as you work towards achieving them.

3. **Practice Gratitude:** Cultivate a gratitude mindset by appreciating the present moment and acknowledging the blessings in your life. Gratitude enhances your overall well-being and helps you find meaning in everyday experiences.

4. **Embrace Challenges:** Embrace challenges as opportunities for growth and learning. View setbacks as stepping stones towards personal development and use them to strengthen your resilience and determination.

5. **Connect with Others:** Foster meaningful connections with like-minded individuals who share your values and aspirations. Surround yourself with a supportive community that encourages personal growth and helps you stay accountable to living a meaningful life.

Benefits of Living a Meaningful Life.

1. **Enhanced Well-being:** Living a meaningful life contributes to overall well-being, leading to greater happiness, satisfaction, and a sense of fulfillment.

2. **Increased Resilience:** The pursuit of meaning builds resilience, allowing you to bounce back from setbacks and navigate challenges with greater strength and perseverance.

3. **Deeper Relationships:** Living a meaningful life strengthens your relationships by fostering deeper connections and a sense of belonging with others who share your values and purpose.

4. **Personal Growth:** A meaningful life provides continuous opportunities for personal growth, self-discovery, and the development of new skills and strengths.

5. **Positive Impact:** By living a meaningful life, you have the potential to make a positive impact on others and the world around you, leaving a lasting legacy that aligns with your values and purpose.

Functions of Living a Meaningful Life.

1. **Sense of Purpose:** Living a meaningful life provides a sense of purpose and direction, guiding your choices and actions toward what truly matters to you.

2. **Source of Motivation:** Meaning serves as a powerful motivator, fueling your drive and determination to pursue your goals and overcome obstacles along the way.

3. **Decision-Making Guide:** When faced with choices and dilemmas, a meaningful life acts as a compass, helping you make decisions that align with your values and contribute to your overall sense of purpose.

4. **Source of Inspiration:** Living a meaningful life inspires others to reflect on their purpose and encourages them to live authentically and pursue what brings them joy and fulfillment.

5. **Alignment of Inner and Outer Worlds:** A meaningful life facilitates the alignment of your inner values and beliefs with your external actions and behaviors, creating a harmonious and authentic way of living.

Techniques for Living a Meaningful Life.

1. **Mindfulness:** Practice mindfulness to cultivate a deep awareness of the present moment, allowing you to engage fully in your experiences and find meaning in the simple joys of life.

2. **Self-Compassion:** Develop self-compassion by being kind and forgiving toward yourself. Treat yourself with the same care and understanding you would offer to a loved one, allowing you to embrace imperfections and learn from failures.

3. **Service to Others:** Engage in acts of kindness and service to others. By contributing to the well-being of others, you create a sense of purpose and fulfillment.

4. **Pursuit of Passions:** Identify and pursue your passions. Dedicate time and effort to engage in activities that ignite your enthusiasm and bring you a sense of joy and fulfillment.

5. **Lifelong Learning:** Embrace a mindset of continuous learning and personal growth. Engage in learning new skills, expanding your knowledge, and exploring new perspectives, which adds depth and meaning to your life.

Factors Influencing a Meaningful Life.

1. **Personal Values:** Aligning your life with your core values plays a crucial role in living a meaningful life. When your actions are congruent with your values, you experience a sense of authenticity and purpose.

2. **Relationships:** Meaningful connections with loved ones, friends, and community contribute to a sense of belonging and purpose. Nurturing positive and supportive relationships enriches your journey toward a meaningful life.

3. **Autonomy and Choice:** Having the freedom to make choices that align with your values and aspirations empowers you to shape your life in a meaningful way.

4. **Growth and Contribution:** Personal growth and making a positive impact on others and the world around you are fundamental factors in living a meaningful life. Embracing opportunities for growth and contributing to something greater than yourself adds depth and purpose to your journey.

5. **Resilience:** Building resilience equips you with the ability to overcome challenges and setbacks, allowing you to maintain

your sense of purpose and continue pursuing a meaningful life even in difficult times.

Causes of Living a Meaningful Life.

1. **Self-Reflection and Introspection:** Taking time for self-reflection and introspection helps uncover your values, passions, and purpose, leading to a deeper understanding of what gives your life meaning.

2. **Life Experiences:** Significant life events, milestones, and transformative experiences can trigger a desire for a more meaningful life. These experiences provide opportunities for growth and self-discovery.

3. **Existential Questions:** Reflecting on existential questions, such as the purpose of life or the nature of existence, can lead to a search for meaning and a heightened awareness of the need to live a meaningful life.

4. **Cultural and Social Influences:** Cultural and social factors, including societal norms, values, and expectations, can shape your understanding of what constitutes a meaningful life and influence your choices and actions.

5. **Personal Agency and Choice:** Ultimately, living a meaningful life is a result of personal agency and the choices you make. Your decision to prioritize meaning and take intentional actions towards a meaningful life is a significant cause in itself.

Importance of Living a Meaningful Life.

1. **Personal Fulfillment:** Living a meaningful life brings a deep sense of fulfillment and satisfaction, as it allows individuals to align their actions and choices with their core values and purpose.

2. **Well-being and Happiness:** Research suggests that living a meaningful life is strongly linked to overall well-being and happiness. It provides a deeper sense of contentment and a greater sense of purpose and direction.

3. **Resilience and Inner Strength:** A meaningful life helps individuals develop resilience and inner strength. This enables them to navigate challenges, setbacks, and adversities with determination and a sense of purpose.

4. **Positive Impact on Others:** By living a meaningful life, individuals have the opportunity to positively impact the lives of others. Through acts of kindness, service, and inspiration, they can create a ripple effect of positivity and make a difference in the world.

5. **Legacy and Longevity:** Living a meaningful life allows individuals to leave a lasting legacy, as their actions and contributions continue to inspire and influence others even after they are gone. It adds depth and purpose to one's existence and creates a meaningful narrative for future generations.

Qualities that Contribute to Living a Meaningful Life.

1. **Authenticity:** Being true to oneself and living authentically is a key quality in living a meaningful life. It involves embracing one's values, passions, and beliefs, and aligning one's actions with these core aspects of identity.

2. **Compassion and Empathy:** Cultivating compassion and empathy towards oneself and others enhances the meaningfulness of life. It involves understanding and connecting with the experiences and emotions of others, fostering deeper relationships and a sense of purpose.

3. **Gratitude:** Practicing gratitude cultivates an appreciation for the present moment and the blessings in one's life. It allows individuals to find meaning and joy in everyday experiences and promotes a positive outlook on life.

4. **Resilience:** Developing resilience is crucial in living a meaningful life, as it helps individuals bounce back from setbacks and challenges. Resilience allows for growth, adaptation, and the pursuit of purpose even in the face of adversity.

5. **Reflective Mindset:** Having a reflective mindset involves regularly engaging in self-reflection and introspection. It helps individuals gain clarity about their values, purpose, and the direction they want to take in life, leading to a more meaningful existence.

Framework for Approaching the Journey.

1. **Self-Reflection:** Begin by engaging in self-reflection to gain a deeper understanding of your values, passions, and aspirations. This provides a foundation for living a meaningful life.

2. **Goal Setting:** Set meaningful goals that align with your values and purpose. These goals serve as guideposts and provide direction for your journey.

3. **Action and Implementation:** Take intentional actions that are in line with your values and contribute to your sense of purpose. Implement changes in your daily life that reflect your commitment to living a meaningful life.

4. **Continuous Growth:** Embrace a mindset of continuous growth and learning. Seek opportunities for personal development, expand your knowledge, and explore new experiences that add depth and meaning to your life.

5. **Reflection and Adjustment:** Regularly reflect on your progress, reassess your goals, and make any necessary adjustments. This iterative process allows for growth, adaptation, and the ongoing pursuit of a meaningful life.

Advantages of Living a Meaningful Life.

1. **Fulfillment and Satisfaction:** Living a meaningful life brings a deep sense of fulfillment and satisfaction, as individuals align their actions with their values and purpose, leading to a greater overall sense of contentment.

2. **Increased Resilience:** The pursuit of meaning builds resilience, allowing individuals to navigate challenges and setbacks with greater strength and determination.

3. **Stronger Relationships:** Living a meaningful life fosters deeper connections and a sense of belonging with others who share similar values and purpose, leading to more meaningful and fulfilling relationships.

4. **Personal Growth and Development:** Living a meaningful life provides continuous opportunities for personal growth, self-discovery, and the development of new skills and strengths.

5. **Positive Impact on Others:** By living a meaningful life, individuals have the potential to make a positive impact on the lives of others and contribute to the betterment of their communities and society as a whole.

Disadvantages of Living a Meaningful Life.

1. **Existential Anxiety:** The pursuit of meaning can sometimes lead to existential anxiety as individuals grapple with questions about the purpose and significance of their existence, which may cause moments of confusion or doubt.

2. **Struggles with Balance:** Living a meaningful life often requires time, energy, and effort, which may lead to challenges in balancing various aspects of life, such as work, relationships, and personal well-being.

3. **Potential for Disappointment:** The pursuit of a meaningful life may involve taking risks, trying new things, and setting

ambitious goals. While these endeavors can lead to great fulfillment, they also carry the risk of disappointment or failure.

4. **Challenges in Finding Meaning:** Discovering and defining meaning can be an ongoing process that requires self-reflection, exploration, and experimentation. It may take time and effort to find a sense of purpose that truly resonates with an individual.

5. **Social Pressures and Expectations:** Living a meaningful life may sometimes clash with societal expectations and norms, leading to potential conflicts or resistance from others who may have different perspectives or values.

Chapter 4: The Preconditions for Personal Change.

Unlocking the Potential Within.

Change is an inherent and constant part of human existence, yet it is often met with resistance and hesitation. Personal change, in particular, requires a set of specific conditions to be present for individuals to embark on transformative journeys. Whether it is overcoming deeply ingrained habits, embracing new perspectives, or pursuing personal growth, understanding the preconditions for change becomes crucial. This chapter explores the conditions that must exist before a person can change, delving into the psychological, social, and environmental factors that influence transformation.

1. Self-Awareness and Desire for Change.

The initial precondition for personal change lies within self-awareness and the genuine desire for transformation. Individuals must recognize the need for change in specific areas of their lives and develop a deep understanding of their current state. This section explores the importance of self-reflection, introspection, and acknowledging personal limitations as catalysts for change. It also delves into the role of intrinsic motivation and the desire for self-improvement in driving individuals toward transformative paths.

2. Willingness to Step Out of Comfort Zones.

Change necessitates individuals to step out of their comfort zones and embrace uncertainty. This section examines the importance of cultivating a growth mindset and the willingness to challenge familiar patterns and routines. It explores the fear of the unknown and the role of risk-taking in creating opportunities for personal growth. Additionally, the concept of embracing vulnerability and being open to new experiences is discussed as integral components of personal change.

2. Supportive Social Environment.

Creating a supportive social environment is crucial for personal change to thrive. This section explores the significance of surrounding oneself with individuals who encourage and inspire growth. It delves into the role of positive relationships, such as mentors, friends, and family, in providing emotional support, accountability, and constructive feedback. The influence of social norms, cultural values, and peer pressure on personal change is also examined.

4. Access to Resources and Tools.

Access to resources and tools is another critical precondition for personal change. This section delves into the importance of acquiring knowledge, skills, and information necessary to facilitate transformation. It explores the role of education, self-help resources, therapy, and personal development programs in empowering individuals to embark on their change journeys. The impact of financial resources, time availability, and access to technology is also considered.

5. Commitment and Persistence.

Sustaining personal change requires unwavering commitment and persistence. This section discusses the importance of setting clear goals, developing action plans, and maintaining discipline throughout the change process. It explores the role of self-discipline, patience, and resilience in overcoming setbacks and obstacles. The significance of celebrating small wins and maintaining long-term focus is also examined.

Tips for Personal Change.

1. **Self-Reflection:** Engage in regular self-reflection to gain a deeper understanding of your current state and identify areas for change.
2. **Goal Setting:** Set specific, measurable, achievable, relevant, and time-bound (SMART) goals that align with your desired change.
3. **Seek Support:** Surround yourself with a supportive network of friends, family, or mentors who can provide encouragement, guidance, and accountability.

4. **Continuous Learning:** Invest in personal development by acquiring new knowledge, skills, and resources that can facilitate your desired change.

5. **Practice Self-Compassion:** Be kind and forgiving towards yourself during the change process. Embrace setbacks as learning opportunities and celebrate small wins along the way.

Benefits of Personal Change.

1. **Personal Growth:** Personal change allows for continuous growth, self-improvement, and the development of new skills and strengths.

2. **Enhanced Well-being:** Positive changes can lead to improved physical, emotional, and mental well-being, resulting in greater overall life satisfaction.

3. **Increased Self-Awareness:** Engaging in personal change encourages self-reflection and introspection, leading to a deeper understanding of oneself and one's values.

4. **Improved Relationships:** Personal change can positively impact relationships by fostering better communication, empathy, and understanding.

5. **Achievement of Goals:** By embracing personal change, individuals are more likely to achieve their desired goals and aspirations, leading to a sense of accomplishment and fulfillment.

Functions of Personal Change.

1. **Breaking Limiting Patterns:** Personal change helps individuals break free from limiting beliefs, habits, and behaviors that hinder personal growth and success.

2. **Adaptation and Resilience:** Change enables individuals to adapt to new circumstances and bounce back from challenges, fostering resilience and the ability to navigate life's ups and downs.

3. **Self-Transformation:** Personal change allows individuals to transform themselves by aligning their actions, beliefs, and values with their desired outcomes.

4. **Empowerment:** Embracing personal change empowers individuals to take control of their lives, make intentional choices, and create positive change in themselves and their environments.

5. **Personal Fulfillment:** Personal change serves as a pathway to personal fulfillment by living a life that is more aligned with one's passions, values, and purpose.

Techniques for Personal Change.

1. **Cognitive Restructuring:** Challenge and modify negative or limiting thought patterns through techniques such as cognitive-behavioral therapy or positive affirmations.

2. **Behavior Modification:** Use strategies like goal-setting, habit formation, and reinforcement to replace old habits with new, desired behaviors.

3. **Mindfulness and Meditation:** Cultivate present-moment awareness and develop a non-judgmental attitude towards thoughts and emotions, promoting self-reflection and positive change.

4. **Visualization and Imagery:** Use visualization techniques to mentally rehearse and reinforce desired outcomes, enhancing motivation and belief in the possibility of change.

5. **Social Support and Accountability:** Engage with supportive individuals, join groups or communities, and enlist an accountability partner to provide encouragement, feedback, and assistance throughout the change process.

Factors Influencing Personal Change.

1. **Motivation:** The level of intrinsic and extrinsic motivation towards change plays a significant role in determining an individual's willingness to embark on and sustain the change process.

2. **Self-Efficacy:** Belief in one's ability to successfully enact change affects the likelihood of initiating and persisting with personal change efforts.

3. **Environmental Influences:** The social, cultural, and physical environment can either support or hinder personal change by providing resources, role models, and opportunities for growth or presenting barriers and limitations.

4. **Past Experiences and Learning:** Previous experiences, successes, and failures shape an individual's beliefs,

expectations, and attitudes toward change, influencing their willingness to engage in further personal transformation.

5. **Emotional Well-being:** Emotional factors such as self-esteem, resilience, and emotional regulation can impact an individual's capacity to navigate challenges, setbacks, and emotional barriers during the change process.

Causes of Personal Change.

1. **Dissatisfaction or Discomfort:** Feeling dissatisfied or uncomfortable with one's current situation or circumstances can catalyze personal change, motivating individuals to seek improvement and growth.

2. **Life Events and Transitions:** Significant life events such as career changes, relationship changes, or major milestones can trigger personal reflection and the desire for change.

3. **External Influence and Inspiration:** Exposure to inspiring stories, role models, or influential individuals can ignite a sense of inspiration and aspiration for personal change.

4. **Internal Reflection and Insight:** Introspection, self-reflection, and a deep exploration of personal values, beliefs, and desires can lead to profound insights and a readiness for personal change.

5. **Desire for Personal Growth and Fulfillment:** An innate yearning for personal growth, self-actualization, and a desire to live a more fulfilling life can drive individuals towards embracing personal change as a means to achieve these goals.

Importance of unlocking your potential and achieving personal growth.

1. **Self-awareness:** Understanding your current situation, strengths, weaknesses, and aspirations is essential for change.
2. **Motivation:** Having a strong desire and drive to make a change will give you the necessary energy to overcome obstacles.
3. **Commitment:** Being dedicated and willing to put in the effort required to achieve personal growth is vital.
4. **Open-mindedness:** Being receptive to new ideas, perspectives, and feedback enables you to broaden your horizons.
5. **Resilience:** Building resilience helps you bounce back from setbacks and stay determined on your journey.

Qualities of unlocking your potential and achieving personal growth.

1. **Self-reflection:** Engaging in introspection and evaluating your thoughts, emotions, and actions promotes self-development.
2. **Adaptability:** Being flexible and adaptable allows you to adjust your approach and learn from different experiences.
3. **Growth mindset:** Embracing challenges, learning from failures, and believing in your ability to develop boosts personal change.

4. **Emotional intelligence:** Developing emotional awareness and managing your own emotions enhances personal growth.

5. **Perseverance:** Showing persistence and determination in the face of obstacles is essential for personal transformation.

The framework of unlocking your potential and achieving personal growth.

1. **Goal setting:** Clearly defining your goals provides a roadmap for personal change and enables you to track your progress.

2. **Action plan:** Breaking down your goals into actionable steps helps you make progress and stay focused.

3. **Support system:** Surrounding yourself with a network of supportive individuals who encourage and motivate you aids personal change.

4. **Continuous learning:** Engaging in self-education, seeking new knowledge and skills, and staying curious facilitate personal growth.

5. **Evaluation and adaptation:** Regularly assessing your progress, learning from challenges, and adjusting your approach ensures effectiveness in personal change efforts.

Advantages of the Preconditions for Personal Change.

1. **Personal growth:** Engaging in personal change allows you to discover and unlock your full potential, leading to self-improvement and personal development.

2. **Increased self-awareness:** Through the preconditions for personal change, you gain a deeper understanding of yourself, your values, and your goals.

3. **Improved resilience:** Facing challenges and overcoming obstacles during personal change builds resilience and the ability to cope with adversity.

4. **Enhanced relationships:** Adopting personal change can lead to improved communication skills, empathy, and understanding, strengthening your relationships with others.

5. **Greater fulfillment:** When you unlock your potential and achieve personal growth, you experience a sense of fulfillment and satisfaction.

Disadvantages of the Preconditions for Personal Change.

1. **Resistance and discomfort:** Personal change often requires stepping out of your comfort zone, which can be challenging and uncomfortable.

2. **Fear of failure:** The fear of failure and making mistakes can hinder progress and discourage individuals from pursuing personal change.

3. **Uncertainty and ambiguity:** Personal change involves entering new territories and embracing the unknown, which can be intimidating.

4. **Time and effort:** Achieving personal change requires consistent effort and dedication, which may be demanding and time-consuming.

5. **Lack of support:** The absence of a supportive environment or a network of like-minded individuals can make personal change more difficult to sustain.

Chapter 5: The Motivational Force of Goals.

Unveiling the Journey of Protagonists.

Goals serve as powerful driving forces that propel individuals toward their desired destinations. Throughout history, countless stories have depicted protagonists who are fueled by their goals, embarking on transformative journeys that shape their character and define their narratives. In this chapter, we will delve into the profound relationship between goals and protagonists, exploring how these aspirations ignite motivation, guide actions, and ultimately contribute to the development of compelling narratives. By examining key literary and cinematic examples, we will unravel the intricate dynamics that make goals a driving force for protagonists.

1. The Essence of Goals.

Goals, at their core, represent the aspirations, desires, and dreams that individuals strive to achieve. They provide a sense of purpose and direction, acting as beacons of light amidst the vast sea of possibilities. By setting goals, protagonists establish a tangible endpoint that becomes the focal point of their journey. Whether it is achieving personal growth, acquiring knowledge, attaining social recognition, or overcoming adversity, goals offer a sense of meaning and fulfillment to protagonists.

2. The Motivational Impetus of Goals.

Goals possess an inherent motivational power that drives protagonists to take action. They serve as catalysts for change, pushing characters beyond their comfort zones and propelling them forward. The pursuit of goals instills a sense of determination, resilience, and perseverance in protagonists, enabling them to overcome obstacles and endure hardships along their journey. The clarity of purpose that goals provide fuels the protagonist's motivation, serving as a constant reminder of why they embarked on their quest in the first place.

3. Goals as Plot Device.

In literature and cinema, goals often serve as crucial plot devices that shape the narrative arc. They act as pivotal moments that set the story in motion, driving the protagonist towards a series of challenges and conflicts. The protagonist's goal becomes the focal point around which the plot revolves, creating tension and suspense as they face numerous obstacles and setbacks. The pursuit of their goal forms the backbone of the story, engaging the audience and propelling the narrative forward.

4. Transformative Journeys.

As protagonists navigate the treacherous path towards their goals, they undergo profound transformations. The pursuit of their aspirations forces them to confront their fears, confront their limitations, and embrace personal growth. Through adversity and triumph, protagonists evolve and develop, emerging as changed individuals by the end of their journey. Goals serve as catalysts for self-discovery and transformation, allowing protagonists to unlock their true potential and realize their deepest desires.

5. The Complex Nature of Goals.

While goals provide motivation and direction to protagonists, they can also be a source of internal conflict and moral dilemmas. As protagonists strive to achieve their goals, they may face ethical challenges or make difficult choices that test their values. This internal struggle adds depth and complexity to their character, making them relatable and human. The journey towards a goal is not always straightforward, and the obstacles encountered along the way force protagonists to confront their vulnerabilities and learn valuable lessons about themselves and the world around them.

Tips for Harnessing the Motivational Force of Goals.

1. **Be Specific and Clear:** Set clear and specific goals that are well-defined. This clarity will provide a sense of direction and focus, allowing you to channel your energy and efforts toward achieving your objectives.

2. **Break Down Goals into Milestones:** Divide your goals into smaller, achievable milestones. This approach helps to create a sense of progress and accomplishment along the way, keeping you motivated and engaged throughout your journey.

3. **Set Challenging yet Attainable Goals:** Strive for goals that push you out of your comfort zone and encourage personal growth. While it's important to challenge yourself, ensure that your goals are realistic and attainable, as unrealistic expectations can lead to frustration and demotivation.

4. **Stay Persistent and Resilient:** Expect obstacles and setbacks along the way. The path toward achieving your goals may not always be smooth, but perseverance and resilience are key to overcoming challenges. Embrace failures as learning opportunities and remain committed to your goals despite setbacks.

5. **Review and Adjust as Needed:** Regularly review your goals and assess your progress. Be open to adjusting your approach if necessary, as circumstances and priorities may change. Flexibility and adaptability are important qualities that allow you to stay motivated and aligned with your evolving aspirations.

Benefits of Setting Goals.

1. **Increased Motivation:** Goals provide a sense of purpose and direction, igniting motivation and driving individuals to take action. They act as a constant reminder of what one is working towards, keeping motivation levels high.

2. **Enhanced Focus and Clarity:** Setting goals helps individuals gain clarity about their priorities and aspirations. This clarity enables them to focus their time, energy, and resources on activities that align with their goals, leading to increased efficiency and productivity.

3. **Personal Growth and Development:** Goals serve as catalysts for personal growth and development. By striving towards goals, individuals challenge themselves, acquire new skills, and expand their knowledge and abilities. This continuous growth contributes to a sense of fulfillment and self-improvement.

4. **Improved Decision-Making:** Goals provide a framework for decision-making. When individuals have a clear understanding of their goals, it becomes easier to make choices that align with their long-term objectives. This clarity minimizes indecisiveness and empowers individuals to make informed decisions.

5. **Sense of Achievement and Satisfaction:** Accomplishing goals brings a sense of achievement and satisfaction. Whether it's reaching a milestone or attaining the ultimate goal, these accomplishments boost self-confidence and provide a sense of fulfillment, reinforcing the motivation to set and pursue new goals.

Functions of Goals.

1. **Direction and Guidance:** Goals provide individuals with a sense of direction and guidance, serving as a compass for

their actions and decisions. They give purpose and meaning to daily activities, ensuring that efforts are aligned with desired outcomes.

2. **Measurement and Evaluation:** Goals act as benchmarks for measuring progress and evaluating performance. By setting specific targets, individuals can objectively assess their achievements and identify areas that require improvement.

3. **Prioritization and Focus:** Goals help individuals prioritize their activities and allocate resources effectively. They enable individuals to identify what is important and allocate time, energy, and resources accordingly, ensuring that efforts are concentrated on the most significant tasks.

4. **Motivation and Inspiration:** Goals serve as powerful sources of motivation and inspiration. They provide individuals with a sense of purpose and drive, fueling their determination to overcome obstacles and persevere in the face of challenges.

5. **Alignment and Coordination:** Goals facilitate alignment and coordination among individuals or teams working towards a common objective. By establishing shared goals, individuals can collaborate effectively, pooling their strengths and resources to achieve collective success.

Techniques for Harnessing the Motivational Force of Goals.

1. **Visualization:** Visualize yourself achieving your goals and immerse yourself in the emotions associated with that

accomplishment. This technique helps create a strong mental image of success, enhancing motivation and focus.

2. **Goal Setting:** Use the SMART (Specific, Measurable, Achievable, Relevant, Time-bound) framework to set well-defined goals. This technique ensures that goals are clear, attainable, and aligned with your aspirations, increasing motivation and providing a clear roadmap.

3. **Accountability:** Share your goals with others or find an accountability partner who can keep you on track. This technique helps create a sense of responsibility and encourages you to stay committed to your goals.

4. **Chunking:** Break down larger goals into smaller, manageable tasks. This technique makes goals less overwhelming, increases a sense of progress, and provides a series of achievable steps that maintain motivation throughout the journey.

5. **Reward System:** Set up a reward system that acknowledges milestones and achievements along the way. This technique reinforces positive behavior, boosts motivation, and provides a sense of satisfaction and enjoyment during the goal pursuit.

Factors Influencing the Motivational Force of Goals.

1. **Intrinsic Motivation:** The inherent desire and enjoyment derived from pursuing a goal can significantly impact motivation. When individuals are intrinsically motivated, their engagement and commitment to the goal increase.

2. **Goal Clarity:** The clarity and specificity of goals play a crucial role in motivation. Clear goals provide a sense of direction, making it easier to visualize success and maintain focus throughout the journey.

3. **Goal Relevance:** The personal relevance and significance of a goal influence motivation. When a goal aligns with an individual's values, interests, and aspirations, it becomes more meaningful and motivational.

4. **Perceived Difficulty:** The perceived difficulty of a goal affects motivation levels. While challenging goals can be motivating, excessively difficult goals may lead to discouragement. Finding the right balance is key to sustaining motivation.

5. **External Support:** The presence of external support systems, such as mentors, coaches, or a supportive network, can positively impact motivation. Encouragement, guidance, and feedback from others can boost motivation and provide a sense of accountability.

Causes of Goal Motivation.

1. **Personal Ambitions:** Individuals are often motivated by their desires, dreams, and aspirations. These internal drives push individuals to set goals and work towards their fulfillment.

2. **External Expectations:** External factors, such as societal expectations, peer pressure, or professional demands, can

drive individuals to set goals. The desire to meet external expectations or gain recognition can be a powerful motivator.

3. **Past Experiences:** Previous successes or failures can significantly influence goal motivation. Positive experiences can inspire individuals to set higher goals, while setbacks may fuel determination to overcome obstacles.

4. **Intrinsic Satisfaction:** The inherent satisfaction derived from the process of pursuing a goal can be a strong motivator. The joy of learning, personal growth, or the fulfillment of a passion can drive individuals to set and strive for goals.

5. **Need for Achievement:** Some individuals possess a strong need for achievement, seeking continuous growth and accomplishment. This intrinsic drive fuels their motivation to set challenging goals and surpass their expectations.

Importance of Goals in the Journey of Protagonists.

1. **Direction and Purpose:** Goals provide a clear sense of direction and purpose to protagonists. They serve as guiding beacons, helping protagonists navigate their journeys and make decisions that align with their ultimate objectives.

2. **Motivation and Drive:** Goals act as powerful motivators, igniting the passion and drive within protagonists. The pursuit of their goals fuels their determination, pushing them to overcome obstacles and persevere even in the face of adversity.

3. **Character Development:** Goals contribute significantly to the development of protagonists' characters. The challenges and obstacles encountered on their journey toward their goals shape their resilience, determination, and personal growth, adding depth and complexity to their narratives.

4. **Conflict and Tension:** Goals introduce conflict and tension into the story, making it engaging and captivating for the audience. The pursuit of goals often involves facing obstacles, encountering adversaries, and dealing with internal struggles, creating a dynamic narrative arc.

5. **Fulfillment and Satisfaction:** Achieving goals brings a sense of fulfillment and satisfaction to protagonists. It provides a sense of accomplishment and validates their efforts, enhancing their satisfaction and contributing to a satisfying narrative resolution.

Qualities of Effective Goals for Protagonists.

1. **Specificity:** Effective goals are specific and well-defined, leaving no room for ambiguity. This clarity enables protagonists to focus their efforts and energies in a targeted manner, increasing their chances of success.

2. **Relevance:** Goals should be relevant to the protagonist's aspirations, values, and the overall story. They should align with the character's motivations and purpose, ensuring that the pursuit of the goal feels authentic and organic.

3. **Challenging yet Attainable:** Goals should be challenging enough to push the protagonist out of their comfort zone and

foster growth, but also realistic and attainable. Strike a balance between ambition and feasibility to maintain motivation and prevent demoralization.

4. **Measurable:** Effective goals are measurable, allowing protagonists to track their progress and evaluate their achievements. This measurement provides a sense of direction and helps protagonists stay on course towards their desired outcomes.

5. **Time-Bound:** Goals should have a timeframe or deadline associated with them. A time-bound aspect creates a sense of urgency and helps protagonists prioritize their actions and allocate their resources effectively.

Frameworks for Setting and Achieving Goals.

1. **SMART Goals:** The SMART (Specific, Measurable, Achievable, Relevant, Time-bound) framework is widely used for goal setting. It ensures that goals are well-defined, realistic, and aligned with the protagonist's overall journey.

2. **OKR (Objectives and Key Results):** The OKR framework involves setting objectives and defining key results that measure progress towards those objectives. It provides a focused approach to goal setting and emphasizes measurable outcomes.

3. **Backward Planning:** In this framework, protagonists start by envisioning their desired outcome and then work backward, mapping out the necessary steps and milestones to

achieve it. This approach helps create a clear roadmap for goal attainment.

4. **GROW Model:** The GROW (Goal, Reality, Options, Will) model is a coaching framework that assists protagonists in defining their goals, assessing their current reality, exploring options, and developing the will and commitment to take action towards their goals.

5. **Kaizen Method:** The Kaizen method emphasizes continuous improvement through small, incremental steps. Protagonists set small, achievable goals and focus on making consistent progress over time, fostering a sense of continuous growth and development.

Advantages of the Motivational Force of Goals for Protagonists.

1. **Clarity and Focus:** Goals provide protagonists with a clear sense of direction and focus. They know what they are working towards, which helps them prioritize their actions and make decisions that align with their objectives.

2. **Motivation and Drive:** Goals act as powerful motivators for protagonists. They fuel their determination and drive, even in the face of obstacles and setbacks. The pursuit of goals keeps them engaged and committed to their journey.

3. **Personal Growth and Development:** Goals encourage personal growth and development for protagonists. They push them out of their comfort zones, challenge their abilities, and provide opportunities for learning and self-improvement.

4. **Resilience and Perseverance:** Goals cultivate resilience and perseverance in protagonists. They learn to overcome obstacles, adapt to adversity, and persist in the face of challenges. This resilience strengthens their character and makes their journey more compelling.

5. **Sense of Achievement and Fulfillment:** Achieving goals brings a sense of accomplishment and fulfillment to protagonists. It validates their efforts, boosts their self-confidence, and provides a satisfying narrative resolution for both the characters and the audience.

Disadvantages of the Motivational Force of Goals for Protagonists.

1. **Tunnel Vision:** Focusing solely on goals can lead to tunnel vision, where protagonists become overly fixated on the result. This narrow focus may cause them to overlook important aspects of their journey or neglect the well-being of themselves and others.

2. **Burnout and Stress:** Pursuing goals relentlessly can lead to burnout and excessive stress for protagonists. The pressure to achieve can take a toll on their mental and physical well-being, potentially compromising their ability to enjoy the journey.

3. **Unrealistic Expectations:** Setting unrealistic goals can set protagonists up for disappointment and demotivation. If the goals are too far-fetched or unattainable, protagonists may feel discouraged and lose faith in their abilities.

4. **Missed Opportunities:** Being solely focused on goals may cause protagonists to overlook valuable opportunities that arise along the way. They may become so fixated on the result that they fail to appreciate the unexpected detours or potential growth that can occur during their journey.

5. **Lack of Adaptability:** Rigidly adhering to goals may hinder protagonists' ability to adapt to changing circumstances or seize new opportunities. They may struggle to adjust their plans or embrace alternative paths that could lead to even greater success or fulfillment.

Chapter 6: A Morning Routine for Directing and Guiding Your Story.

The way we start our day sets the tone for the rest of it. As individuals, we are the authors of our own stories, and it is crucial to have a morning routine that directs and guides our narrative. A well-crafted morning routine not only helps us optimize our physical and mental well-being but also provides a framework for intentional living. In this chapter, we will explore the importance of a morning routine in shaping our personal stories and discuss practical steps to design a routine that aligns with our goals, values, and aspirations.

1. Understanding the Power of a Morning Routine.

- **Setting Intentions:** A morning routine allows us to set clear intentions for the day ahead. By consciously deciding how we want to show up in the world and what we want to accomplish, we take control of our narrative and actively direct the course of our story.

- **Creating Momentum:** Starting the day with a structured routine creates momentum. It helps us build positive habits, establish a rhythm, and propel us forward toward our goals. This momentum sets the stage for productivity and success.
- **Enhancing Well-being:** A morning routine that prioritizes self-care and well-being fosters physical and mental health. Engaging in activities like exercise, meditation, or journaling in the morning promotes a sense of balance, reduces stress, and enhances overall well-being.

2. Elements of an Effective Morning Routine.

- **Reflection and Gratitude:** Taking a few moments for reflection and expressing gratitude can set a positive tone for the day. This can be done through journaling, practicing mindfulness, or simply pausing to appreciate the present moment.
- **Mindfulness or Meditation:** Incorporating mindfulness or meditation practices into the morning routine helps cultivate a calm and focused mind. This can involve breathing exercises, guided meditation, or mindful movement.
- **Physical Activity:** Engaging in physical activity in the morning boosts energy levels, improves mood, and enhances overall health. This can include activities like stretching, yoga, jogging, or any form of exercise that suits individual preferences.
- **Nourishing the Body:** Prioritizing a healthy breakfast that provides essential nutrients nourishes the body and fuels it

for the day. This can involve preparing a nutritious meal or enjoying a balanced breakfast to support overall well-being.

- **Setting Goals:** Taking time to set and review goals in the morning allows us to align our actions with our aspirations. This can involve writing down short-term and long-term goals, creating action plans, or visualizing success.

3. Designing Your Personal Morning Routine.

- **Assessing Individual Needs:** Understanding our unique preferences, energy levels, and priorities helps in crafting a personalized morning routine. This could involve considering whether we are more productive in the morning or evening, identifying activities that energize us, and aligning our routine with our values and goals.

- **Experimentation and Adaptation:** Designing an effective morning routine requires experimentation and adaptation. It is essential to be open to trying different activities and adjusting the routine based on what works best for us. Flexibility allows us to fine-tune our routine to maximize its impact.

- **Time Management:** Allocating sufficient time for each activity within the morning routine is crucial. This involves assessing how much time is needed for each activity and organizing the routine to ensure a balanced and realistic schedule.

- **Consistency and Accountability:** Consistency is key to making a morning routine effective. Setting a regular wake-up time and committing to the routine establishes a sense of discipline and accountability. Sharing our routine with others or finding an accountability partner can further enhance commitment and motivation.

- **Continual Growth and Adaptation:** Our stories evolve, and so should our morning routines. Regularly evaluating and modifying the routine as our goals and priorities change is essential to ensure it remains relevant and supportive of our personal growth and development.

Tips for a Morning Routine that Directs and Guides Your Story.

1. **Set Clear Intentions:** Start your day by setting clear intentions for how you want to show up in the world and what you aim to accomplish. Write down your goals and visualize success to align your actions with your aspirations.

2. **Prioritize Self-Care:** Incorporate activities that prioritize your physical and mental well-being. This can include mindfulness or meditation practices, exercise, or engaging in activities that bring you joy and relaxation.

3. **Reflect and Express Gratitude:** Take a few moments for reflection and express gratitude for the present moment and the opportunities before you. Journaling or engaging in mindfulness exercises can help foster a positive mindset and set a positive tone for the day.

4. **Create a Balanced Schedule:** Design a routine that balances different aspects of your life, such as work, personal growth, relationships, and leisure. Allocate time for each activity,

ensuring that you have a well-rounded approach to your morning routine.

5. **Be Consistent:** Consistency is key to making your morning routine effective. Establish a regular wake-up time and commit to practicing your routine every day. Consistency builds discipline and allows your routine to become a natural part of your daily life.

Benefits of a Morning Routine for Directing and Guiding Your Story.

1. **Increased Productivity:** A well-designed morning routine helps you start the day with focus and purpose, leading to increased productivity throughout the day. By setting clear intentions and engaging in activities that align with your goals, you can make progress toward your aspirations.

2. **Enhanced Well-being:** Prioritizing self-care in your morning routine promotes physical and mental well-being. Mindfulness exercises, exercise, and nourishing your body with a healthy breakfast contribute to overall health, reducing stress, and enhancing your well-being.

3. **Improved Mental Clarity:** Engaging in activities like meditation or reflection in the morning helps clear your mind and improve mental clarity. This allows you to approach your day with a calm and focused mindset, making better decisions and facing challenges with clarity and resilience.

4. **Personal Growth and Self-Development:** By incorporating activities that support personal growth, such as goal-setting

and reflection, your morning routine becomes a catalyst for self-development. Regularly engaging in these practices helps you evolve, learn, and become a better version of yourself.

5. **Emotional Resilience:** A morning routine that includes gratitude and reflection cultivates emotional resilience. By starting the day with a positive mindset, you are better equipped to handle stress, setbacks, and challenges that may arise throughout the day.

Functions of a Morning Routine for Directing and Guiding Your Story.

1. **Setting the Tone:** A morning routine establishes the tone for the rest of your day. It allows you to start on a positive and intentional note, guiding your mindset and approach to the challenges and opportunities that come your way.

2. **Providing Structure:** A well-designed morning routine provides structure and organization to your day. It helps you prioritize tasks and activities, ensuring that you allocate time to what matters most to you and your personal story.

3. **Cultivating Discipline:** By committing to a consistent morning routine, you cultivate discipline in your life. This discipline spills over into other areas, enabling you to stay focused, motivated, and dedicated to achieving your goals.

4. **Aligning Actions with Aspirations:** A morning routine serves as a reminder of your goals and aspirations. By engaging in activities that align with your values and long-

term vision, you ensure that your actions are in harmony with the story you want to create for yourself.

5. **Enhancing Self-Awareness:** Regularly practicing a morning routine helps you develop self-awareness. By reflecting, setting intentions, and checking in with yourself, you become more attuned to your thoughts, emotions, and desires. This self-awareness allows you to make conscious choices that align with your authentic self.

Techniques for a Morning Routine that Directs and Guides Your Story.

1. **Visualization:** Spend a few minutes visualizing your desired outcomes and success. Imagine yourself achieving your goals and living your ideal life. This technique helps align your thoughts and actions with the story you want to create.

2. **Affirmations:** Use positive affirmations to reinforce your beliefs and goals. Repeat affirmations that resonate with you, such as "I am capable of achieving my dreams" or "I am deserving of success." Affirmations help reprogram your subconscious mind and shape your story.

3. **Goal Setting:** Set specific, measurable, achievable, relevant, and time-bound (SMART) goals for the day, week, or month. Break them down into actionable steps and incorporate them into your morning routine. This technique ensures that you are actively working towards your desired outcomes.

4. **Mindfulness or Meditation:** Practice mindfulness or meditation to cultivate a present-moment awareness. Focus

on your breath, sensations, or a mantra to calm your mind and cultivate inner peace. This technique helps you approach your day with clarity, reducing stress and enhancing decision-making.

5. **Gratitude Practice:** Start your day by expressing gratitude for the blessings in your life. Write down or mentally acknowledge things you are grateful for. This technique shifts your focus to the positive and cultivates a mindset of abundance and appreciation.

Factors to Consider for a Morning Routine that Directs and Guides Your Story.

1. **Personal Values:** Align your morning routine with your values. Consider what is most important to you and ensure that your routine reflects those values. This factor ensures that your actions are in harmony with the story you want to create.

2. **Energy Levels:** Take into account your natural energy levels and rhythms. Some individuals are more productive in the morning, while others thrive in the evening. Design your routine to leverage your peak energy periods for optimal performance.

3. **Time Constraints:** Consider the time available in your morning routine and allocate it wisely. Be realistic about what activities you can include and ensure that you have enough time for each one. Factor in other commitments and responsibilities to create a balanced schedule.

4. **Personal Preferences:** Consider activities that resonate with you and bring you joy. Choose activities that you genuinely enjoy and find fulfilling. This factor ensures that your morning routine is sustainable and enjoyable, increasing your motivation to stick with it.

5. **Adaptability:** Recognize that life is dynamic and your routine may need to adapt accordingly. Be open to adjusting your routine as circumstances change or as you evolve in your journey. Being flexible allows you to flow with the changes and stay aligned with your story.

Causes for Establishing a Morning Routine that Directs and Guides Your Story.

1. **Intentional Living:** A morning routine helps you live with intention, ensuring that each day is purposeful and aligned with your desired story. It helps you actively shape your life rather than passively letting life unfold.

2. **Personal Growth:** A well-designed morning routine fosters personal growth and self-improvement. By engaging in activities that promote reflection, goal-setting, and self-care, you continuously evolve and become the best version of yourself.

3. **Focus and Clarity:** A morning routine provides a structured start to your day, enhancing focus and mental clarity. By engaging in mindfulness practices, visualization, and goal-setting, you prime your mind for optimal performance and decision-making.

4. **Emotional Well-being:** Establishing a morning routine that includes gratitude and self-care activities nurtures your emotional well-being. It helps you start the day on a positive note, reducing stress and cultivating a resilient mindset.

5. **Self-Discipline:** A morning routine cultivates self-discipline and strengthens your ability to follow through on commitments. By consistently practicing your routine, you develop discipline in other areas of your life, leading to increased productivity and success.

Importance of a Morning Routine.

1. **Clarity and Focus:** A morning routine helps you start your day with clarity and focus, enabling you to prioritize tasks and make progress toward your goals.

2. **Productivity:** By establishing a structured routine, you enhance productivity and efficiency, ensuring that you make the most of your time and resources.

3. **Emotional Well-being:** A morning routine that includes self-care activities promotes emotional well-being, reducing stress and fostering a positive mindset for the day ahead.

4. **Personal Growth:** Engaging in activities like reflection, goal setting, and learning in your morning routine contributes to personal growth and self-improvement.

5. **Consistency and Discipline:** A consistent morning routine cultivates discipline, allowing you to develop habits and follow through on commitments, which are key to long-term success.

Qualities of an Effective Morning Routine.

1. **Purposeful:** An effective morning routine is designed with a specific purpose in mind, aligning with your values and aspirations.
2. **Balanced:** It includes a balance of activities that address different aspects of your life, such as physical health, mental well-being, personal growth, and relationships.
3. **Customizable:** A good morning routine is flexible and can be tailored to suit your individual needs and preferences, accommodating changes and evolving goals.
4. **Energizing:** It incorporates activities that energize and motivate you, setting a positive tone for the day.
5. **Sustainable:** An effective morning routine is sustainable in the long run, fitting into your lifestyle and allowing for adjustments as needed.

Framework for Designing a Morning Routine.

1. **Set a Clear Intention:** Start your morning routine by setting a clear intention for the day, focusing on what you want to achieve and how you want to show up in the world.
2. **Physical Activity:** Engage in physical activity to energize your body and boost your mood. This can include exercises, stretching, or even a short walk.
3. **Mindfulness or Meditation:** Dedicate time for mindfulness or meditation practices to cultivate mental clarity, reduce stress, and enhance focus.

4. **Personal Growth:** Allocate time for activities that promote personal growth, such as reading, journaling, or learning a new skill. This allows for continuous learning and self-improvement.

5. **Review and Plan:** Reflect on the previous day's accomplishments and challenges, and plan your tasks and priorities for the current day. This helps you stay organized and focused on your goals.

Advantages of a Morning Routine.

1. **Increased Productivity:** A well-designed morning routine helps you start your day with focus and purpose, allowing you to prioritize tasks and accomplish more.

2. **Improved Mental Clarity:** Engaging in activities like meditation or reflection in the morning helps clear your mind, enhance mental clarity, and improve decision-making throughout the day.

3. **Enhanced Well-being:** A morning routine that incorporates self-care activities promotes physical and mental well-being, reducing stress and increasing overall happiness.

4. **Personal Growth:** By dedicating time to activities like goal-setting, learning, and reflection, a morning routine supports personal growth and self-improvement, allowing you to evolve and become the best version of yourself.

5. **Consistency and Discipline:** Following a morning routine cultivates discipline and consistency in your life, helping you

develop habits and stay committed to your goals and aspirations.

Disadvantages of a Morning Routine.

1. **Rigidity:** A strict morning routine can become rigid and inflexible, making it difficult to adapt to changing circumstances or personal needs.

2. **Lack of Spontaneity:** Following a set routine every morning may limit opportunities for spontaneity and creativity, potentially stifling exploration and new experiences.

3. **Pressure to Perform:** A morning routine that focuses heavily on productivity and achievement can create pressure to perform at a high level consistently, leading to stress and burnout.

4. **Time Constraints:** A lengthy morning routine may require waking up earlier, which can be challenging for individuals who struggle with getting enough sleep or have other commitments.

5. **Monotony:** A repetitive morning routine may become monotonous over time, potentially leading to boredom or a lack of motivation to continue with the routine.

II

Part Two

In the journey of life, having a well-defined strategy is crucial to navigate through challenges, capitalize on opportunities, and live a fulfilling and purposeful existence. A strategic life plan serves as a roadmap, guiding individuals toward their goals, aspirations, and personal growth. This part I'll explores the importance of creating a strategy for life and provides a comprehensive framework to develop an effective life strategy.

Crafting a Strategic Life Plan.

In the journey of life, having a well-defined strategy is crucial to navigate through challenges, capitalize on opportunities, and live a fulfilling and purposeful existence. A strategic life plan serves as a roadmap, guiding individuals toward their goals, aspirations, and personal growth. This part I'll explores the importance of creating a strategy for life and provides a comprehensive framework to develop an effective life strategy.

1. Understanding the Significance of a Life Strategy.

- Defining a life strategy.
- Benefits of having a life strategy.
- Clarity and direction.
- Goal achievement and progress.
- Adaptability and resilience.

2. Reflection and Self-Assessments.

- Identifying personal values and passions.
- Assessing strengths and weaknesses.

- Defining short-term and long-term goals.

3. Goal Setting.

- SMART goal framework.
- Prioritizing goals.
- Breaking down goals into actionable steps.

4. Creating a Personal Development Plan.

- Identifying areas for growth and improvement.
- Establishing a plan for acquiring new skills and knowledge.
- Continuous learning and self-improvement.

5. Time Management and Productivity.

- Assessing time allocation and identifying time-wasting activities.
- Developing effective time management strategies.
- Enhancing productivity through prioritization and focus.

6. Building a Support Network.

- Identifying mentors, role models, and advisors.
- Cultivating meaningful relationships.
- Leveraging networks for personal and professional growth.

7. Embracing Adaptability and Resilience.

- Recognizing the inevitability of change.

- Developing resilience to overcome setbacks.
- Embracing opportunities for growth and adaptation.

8. Regular Evaluation and Revision.

- Assessing progress towards goals.
- Adjusting strategies to align with changing circumstances.
- Celebrating achievements and learning from failures.

Chapter 7: The Power of Eulogies.

Reflecting on Life's Journey.

A eulogy, traditionally delivered at a person's funeral, is a profound opportunity to reflect on the entirety of one's life as the central figure. While typically associated with the end of life, the act of crafting a eulogy offers a unique chance for introspection and self-discovery. This chapter delves into the significance of eulogies as a means of personal reflection and explores how this process allows individuals to examine their lives, celebrate their accomplishments, and contemplate their impact on others.

1. Understanding the Purpose of a Eulogy.

- Definition and historical context.
- Symbolic representation of a life story.
- Honoring and remembering the deceased.

2. The Role of Reflection in Personal Growth.

- Introspection and self-awareness.
- Gaining insights from past experiences.
- Recognizing personal growth and change.

3. Crafting a Eulogy: Unveiling Your Life's Narrative.

- Collecting memories and anecdotes.
- Identifying key themes and values.
- Presenting a coherent narrative.

4. Celebrating Accomplishments and Milestones.

- Recognizing personal achievements.
- Acknowledging contributions to society.
- Highlighting moments of impact and significance.

5. Evaluating Relationships and Connections.

- Assessing the impact on others' lives.
- Expressing gratitude and appreciation.
- Examining the quality of relationships.

6. Contemplating Legacy and Purpose.

- Reflecting on a life's purpose and meaning.
- Examining the imprint left on the world.
- Identifying opportunities for growth and fulfillment.

7. Embracing Lessons and Growth Opportunities.

- Learning from failures and challenges.
- Identifying areas for personal development.
- Committing to ongoing growth and self-improvement.

8. The Transformative Power of Eulogies.

- Providing closure and healing.
- Inspiring others through personal narratives.

C. Encouraging proactive living and intentional choices.

9. Applying Eulogical Reflection to Daily Life.

- Incorporating self-reflection practices.
- Setting goals aligned with values and purpose.
- Embracing the present and living with intention.

Tips for Crafting a Powerful Eulogy.

1. **Gather Memories and Anecdotes:** Collect meaningful stories, memories, and anecdotes that capture the essence of the individual's life. These personal narratives offer a unique perspective and provide a rich foundation for the eulogy's content.

2. **Identify Key Themes and Values:** Reflect on the person's core values, passions, and beliefs. Identify the overarching themes that defined their life and weave them into the eulogy's narrative, showcasing their true character and spirit.

3. **Balance Honesty and Compassion:** While it is essential to be honest and authentic in portraying the individual's life, approach the eulogy with compassion and sensitivity. Strike a balance between honoring their achievements and acknowledging their imperfections.

4. **Engage the Audience:** Craft the eulogy in a way that resonates with the audience. Use storytelling techniques, humor, and heartfelt emotions to engage and connect with the listeners, allowing them to feel a deeper connection to the person being eulogized.

5. **Practice and Delivery:** Practice the eulogy beforehand to ensure a smooth and confident delivery. Pay attention to pacing, tone, and body language, and allow for pauses that allow the audience to reflect on the shared memories and emotions.

Benefits of Eulogies for Personal Reflection.

1. **Self-Awareness and Introspection:** Crafting a eulogy prompts deep introspection, leading to a heightened sense of self-awareness. It encourages individuals to reflect on their values, purpose, and the impact they want to have on others' lives.

2. **Celebration of Accomplishments:** Eulogies provide a platform to celebrate the individual's achievements, both big and small. They allow for the recognition of personal growth, milestones, and the positive contributions made throughout life.

3. **Healing and Closure:** The act of delivering or listening to a eulogy offers a cathartic experience for mourners. It provides an opportunity for healing, closure, and the expression of emotions in a supportive environment.

4. **Commemoration of Relationships:** Eulogies honor the relationships that the individual cultivated throughout their life. They allow for the expression of gratitude, appreciation, and the sharing of cherished memories, strengthening the bond between the deceased and the living.

5. **Inspiration and Legacy:** Eulogies serve as a source of inspiration for the audience, reminding them of the importance of living a purposeful life. They encourage individuals to reflect on their legacies, fostering a desire for personal growth and leaving a positive impact on the world.

Functions of Eulogies.

1. **Remembering and Honoring the Deceased:** Eulogies provide a platform to remember and honor the life of the deceased. They serve as a tribute to their accomplishments, character, and the impact they had on others.

2. **Storytelling and Narrative Creation:** Eulogies help construct a narrative that encapsulates the individual's life story. They weave together memories, anecdotes, and experiences, allowing the audience to connect with and understand the person on a deeper level.

3. **Community and Unity Building:** Eulogies bring people together in grief, fostering a sense of community and unity.

They provide a space for collective mourning and the sharing of memories, offering solace and support to those in attendance.

4. **Reflection and Contemplation:** Eulogies prompt reflection and contemplation on the brevity of life and the importance of cherishing relationships. They encourage individuals to consider their mortality and make the most of their time on Earth.

5. **Legacy Preservation:** Eulogies contribute to the preservation of the individual's legacy. By sharing stories and memories, they ensure that the person's impact and contributions are remembered for generations to come.

Techniques for Crafting Powerful Eulogies.

1. **Storytelling:** Engage the audience through storytelling techniques, using vivid descriptions, anecdotes, and narratives to bring the person's life to life. Create a compelling narrative that captures the essence of their journey.

2. **Personalization:** Tailor the eulogy to reflect the unique qualities and experiences of the individual being eulogized. Share specific memories, achievements, and traits that highlight their distinct personality and impact.

3. **Emotional Appeal:** Evoke emotions in the audience through sincere expressions. Share personal experiences, express gratitude, and convey the depth of the relationship with the

deceased, creating a meaningful connection with the listeners.

4. **Balance:** Strike a balance between celebrating the person's accomplishments and acknowledging their challenges and flaws. Present a well-rounded portrait that captures the complexities of their life, showcasing their growth and resilience.

5. **Authenticity:** Be genuine to yourself when delivering the eulogy. Speak from the heart, using one's voice and emotions, to convey a heartfelt tribute that resonates with the audience.

Factors Contributing to the Power of Eulogies.

1. **Emotional Connection:** Eulogies have the power to create a strong emotional bond between the eulogist, the audience, and the memories of the deceased. The shared experience of grief and remembrance fosters a deep sense of connection and understanding.

2. **Reflection and Contemplation:** Eulogies encourage reflection and contemplation on the brevity of life, the value of relationships, and the importance of personal growth. They prompt individuals to ponder their own lives and make meaningful choices.

3. **Communal Support:** Eulogies provide a space for communal support and healing. They bring together friends, family, and community members, allowing them to share their grief, memories, and support for one another.

4. **Legacy and Impact:** Eulogies highlight the impact that the deceased had on others' lives, emphasizing their legacy and contributions. They inspire others to consider their legacies and motivate them to live purposefully.

5. **Celebration of Life:** Eulogies serve as a celebration of the person's life and accomplishments. They allow for the sharing of joyful memories, achievements, and the positive impact they have on individuals and communities.

Causes of the Power of Eulogies.

1. **Remembrance and Tribute:** Eulogies serve as a means to remember and pay tribute to the life and legacy of the deceased. They provide an opportunity to honor their memory and preserve their stories for future generations.

2. **Healing and Closure:** Eulogies contribute to the healing process by providing a space for expressing grief and emotions. They offer closure, allowing mourners to say goodbye and find solace in shared memories and support.

3. **Sense of Identity:** Eulogies help individuals reflect on their own identity and values. They prompt introspection and encourage individuals to consider how they want to be remembered and the impact they want to have on others.

4. **Sense of Community:** Eulogies foster a sense of community and connection among those in attendance. They bring people together in a shared experience of mourning, providing comfort, support, and a sense of belonging.

5. **Inspiration and Motivation:** Eulogies inspire and motivate individuals to live more purposefully. They remind people of the fragility of life and encourage them to make the most of their time, fostering personal growth and positive change.

Importance of Eulogies in Reflecting on Life's Journey.

1. **Celebration of Life:** Eulogies offer a unique opportunity to celebrate and honor the life of the deceased. They allow for the recognition of their accomplishments, values, and the positive impact they have on others, fostering a sense of appreciation and gratitude.

2. **Reflection and Introspection:** Eulogies prompt individuals to reflect upon their own lives. They encourage introspection, inspiring individuals to contemplate their values, purpose, and the legacy they wish to leave behind, igniting personal growth and self-awareness.

3. **Healing and Closure:** Eulogies serve as a means of healing and closure for mourners. They provide a safe space for expressing grief, sharing memories, and finding solace in the support of others, facilitating the emotional healing process.

4. **Connection and Unity:** Eulogies bring people together in a shared experience of remembrance. They create a sense of unity and community, strengthening relationships and fostering connections between family, friends, and loved ones.

5. **Inspiration and Motivation:** Eulogies inspire and motivate individuals to live purposefully. They serve as a reminder of

the brevity of life, urging individuals to make the most of their time and encouraging them to pursue their passions and aspirations.

Qualities that Make Eulogies Impactful.

1. **Authenticity:** A powerful eulogy is authentic and genuine. It reflects the true essence of the deceased, capturing their personality, values, and unique qualities, allowing the audience to connect on a deeper level.

2. **Emotional Resonance:** Eulogies evoke emotions in the audience. They convey heartfelt stories, memories, and sentiments, creating a profound emotional resonance that leaves a lasting impact on the listeners.

3. **Storytelling:** Eulogies employ storytelling techniques to engage the audience and bring the deceased's life to life. They weave together narratives, anecdotes, and experiences, creating a compelling and meaningful narrative arc.

4. **Balance:** A well-crafted eulogy strikes a balance between celebrating the person's accomplishments and acknowledging their challenges and flaws. It presents a holistic view of their life, honoring their achievements while recognizing their humanity.

5. **Connection to the Audience:** A powerful eulogy connects with the audience on a personal level. It speaks to the shared experiences, memories, and emotions, fostering a sense of empathy and understanding among the listeners.

Frameworks for Crafting Eulogies.

1. **Chronological:** Chronologically organize the eulogy, starting from the person's early life and progressing through significant milestones, achievements, and experiences, showcasing their journey over time.

2. **Thematic:** Structure the eulogy around key themes that define the person's life. Identify their passions, values, and contributions, and present them in a coherent and organized manner, highlighting the impact of these themes.

3. **Relationship-based:** Focus on the relationships the deceased had with others. Share stories, anecdotes, and memories that reflect the depth and significance of these connections, emphasizing the love, support, and impact they had on others.

4. **Values-driven:** Craft the eulogy around the person's core values. Identify the values that guided their life, and illustrate how they lived in alignment with these values, inspiring others to reflect on their values and choices.

5. **Collaborative:** Involve others in the creation of the eulogy. Seek input from family, friends, and loved ones to gather diverse perspectives and memories. Incorporate their contributions to create a comprehensive and inclusive tribute.

Advantages of Eulogies.

1. **Celebration of Life:** Eulogies allow for the celebration of the deceased's life and achievements. They provide a meaningful way to honor their memory, share stories, and

highlight their positive impact on others, fostering a sense of appreciation and gratitude.

2. **Healing and Closure:** Eulogies contribute to the healing process by providing a space for expressing grief and emotions. They offer closure, allowing mourners to say goodbye and find solace in shared memories and support, facilitating emotional healing.

3. **Reflection and Introspection:** Eulogies prompt individuals to reflect upon their own lives. They encourage introspection, inspiring individuals to contemplate their values, purpose, and the legacy they wish to leave behind, fostering personal growth and self-awareness.

4. **Communal Support:** Eulogies bring together friends, family, and community members, providing a space for communal support and connection. They allow mourners to share their grief, memories, and support for one another, strengthening relationships and fostering a sense of belonging.

5. **Inspiration and Motivation:** Eulogies inspire and motivate individuals to live purposefully. They serve as a reminder of the brevity of life, urging individuals to make the most of their time and encouraging them to pursue their passions and aspirations.

Disadvantages of Eulogies.

1. **Emotional Distress:** Eulogies can evoke intense emotions, potentially causing distress for mourners who are already

grieving. The emotional weight of the eulogy may be overwhelming for some individuals, leading to heightened sadness or discomfort.

2. **Unfulfilled Expectations:** Eulogies may not meet the expectations of all attendees. Different individuals may have their perceptions and desires for how the eulogy should be delivered, potentially resulting in disappointment or dissatisfaction.

3. **Inequality of Attention:** Eulogies may inadvertently shine a spotlight on certain aspects of the deceased's life or relationships, potentially overlooking or downplaying other significant aspects. This inequality of attention can lead to feelings of exclusion or unfulfilled representation.

4. **Pressure on the Eulogist:** Delivering a eulogy can be emotionally challenging and intimidating for the eulogist. The pressure to accurately represent the deceased's life and convey their impact effectively can be overwhelming, potentially leading to added stress or anxiety.

5. **Time Constraints:** Eulogies are often delivered within a limited timeframe, typically during a funeral or memorial service. This time constraint may restrict the comprehensive portrayal of the deceased's life and limit the depth of reflection and storytelling.

Chapter 8: A Decent Eulogy.

Celebrating Love for People and Things as Protagonists.

Eulogies offer a unique opportunity to honor and remember the life of a loved one who has passed away. A decent eulogy goes beyond highlighting the deceased's achievements and characteristics; it delves into the depths of their love for people and things. Love is a powerful force that shapes our lives and relationships, and discussing the people and things that the protagonists loved in a eulogy can provide a profound understanding of their values, passions, and impact. In this essay, we will explore the significance of discussing love in a eulogy, how it reflects the essence of the deceased, and the importance of celebrating and preserving these cherished connections.

1. Love for People.

- **Family and Relationships:**
- Discussing the love the protagonists had for their family members: parents, siblings, spouse, children, etc.

- Highlighting their devotion, care, and sacrifices for their loved ones.
- Sharing heartwarming anecdotes and memories that exemplify their love for family.
- **Friends and Companions:**
- Exploring the deep friendships and meaningful connections the protagonists cultivated.
- Describing the support, loyalty, and joy they shared with their friends.
- Narrating stories that capture the essence of these friendships and the impact they had on the protagonists' lives.
- **Community and Society:**
- Examining the protagonists' love for their community and society.
- Discussing their involvement in philanthropic activities, volunteer work, or social causes.
- Highlighting the positive contributions they made to the lives of others and the broader community.

2. Love for Things.

- **Passion and Hobbies:**
- Exploring the protagonists' passions and hobbies that brought them joy and fulfillment.
- Discussing their commitment to their craft, whether it be music, art, sports, or any other pursuit.
- Sharing stories and experiences that showcase the protagonists' dedication and love for their chosen pursuits.

- **Nature and Environment:**
- Examining the protagonists' love for nature and the environment.
- Describing their appreciation for the beauty of the natural world and their efforts to protect it.
- Narrating instances where the protagonists actively engaged in environmental conservation or sustainable practices.
- **Intellectual Pursuits:**
- Discussing the protagonists' love for knowledge, learning, and intellectual pursuits.
- Highlighting their curiosity, thirst for knowledge, and engagement in academia or intellectual communities.
- Sharing stories that illustrate the protagonists' commitment to intellectual growth and their impact in their respective fields.

3. Reflection and Impact.

- **Personal Growth and Inspiration:**
- Reflecting on how the protagonists' love for people and things contributed to their personal growth.
- Discussing how their love inspired others and motivated them to live more purposefully.
- Exploring the legacy of love they left behind and the impact it continues to have on others.
- **Lessons Learned:**
- Extracting valuable lessons from the protagonists' love for people and things.

- Discussing how their love can serve as a guide for others in their own lives.
- Emphasizing the importance of cherishing relationships and pursuing passions.
- **Celebration and Preservation:**
- Stressing the significance of celebrating the love the protagonists had for people and things.
- Exploring ways to preserve their memory and the legacy of their love.
- Discussing the role of eulogies in ensuring that the love they shared continues to inspire and resonate with others.

Conclusion.

A decent eulogy goes beyond the surface-level attributes of the deceased and delves into the deep love they had for people and things. By discussing the people they loved, such as family, friends, and the broader community, and the things that brought them joy and fulfillment, such as passions, nature, and intellectual pursuits, we gain a comprehensive understanding of their values and impact. Love serves as the foundation of our relationships and the driving force behind our passions. Celebrating this love in a eulogy allows us to honor the deceased in a meaningful and authentic way, while also inspiring others to cherish their connections and pursue their passions. In preserving the memory of the protagonists' love, we ensure that their legacy continues to resonate and shape the lives of those they touched. A decent eulogy celebrates the power of love and its enduring impact on the journey of life.

Tips for Crafting a Decent Eulogy.

1. **Reflect on Relationships:** Take time to reflect on the relationships the deceased cherished. Consider their connection with family, friends, and community members. Incorporate anecdotes and memories that highlight the depth of these relationships and the love shared.

2. **Explore Passions and Hobbies:** Identify the passions and hobbies that brought joy and fulfillment to the deceased. Discuss how these pursuits enriched their life and impacted others. Share stories that illustrate their dedication and love for these activities.

3. **Capture Meaningful Moments:** Remember and capture the meaningful moments the deceased had with loved ones and cherished things. Share stories and experiences that reflect the profound impact these moments had on their life and relationships.

4. **Express Gratitude:** Express gratitude for the love the deceased had for people and things. Acknowledge the positive influence they had on others' lives and the gratitude felt for their presence. Use the eulogy as an opportunity to express heartfelt appreciation.

5. **Create a Narrative Arc:** Craft the eulogy with a narrative arc that weaves together the love for people and things. Organize the content in a way that flows seamlessly and engages the audience. Ensure a balance between personal anecdotes, reflections, and celebrations of love.

Benefits of Celebrating Love for People and Things in a Eulogy.

1. **Honoring the Deceased:** By celebrating the love the deceased had for people and things, the eulogy pays homage to their authentic selves. It acknowledges their passions, relationships, and the impact they had on others, ensuring their memory lives on.

2. **Providing Comfort and Closure:** Focusing on love provides comfort and closure to grieving individuals. It reminds them of the cherished relationships and shared experiences, allowing them to find solace in the memories and love they shared with the deceased.

3. **Inspiring Reflection and Appreciation:** A eulogy that celebrates love catalyzes reflection. It prompts individuals to contemplate their relationships and passions, inspiring them to cherish their loved ones and pursue their dreams wholeheartedly.

4. **Strengthening Connections:** By highlighting the love the deceased had for people and things, the eulogy strengthens the connections between family, friends, and the larger community. It fosters a sense of unity, support, and shared appreciation for the impact of love in our lives.

5. **Leaving a Lasting Legacy:** Celebrating love in a eulogy ensures that the legacy of the deceased lives on. It serves as a testament to the love they shared and the impact they had, inspiring future generations to embrace love and cherish their relationships and passions.

Functions of a Eulogy that Celebrates Love for People and Things.

1. **Commemoration:** A eulogy celebrates the life and love of the deceased, honoring their memory and legacy. It reminds everyone of the impact they had on others and the love they shared.

2. **Reflection:** A eulogy prompts individuals to reflect on their relationships and passions, encouraging personal growth, gratitude, and self-awareness.

3. **Healing:** By focusing on love, a eulogy provides emotional healing and closure to grieving individuals. It offers comfort, support, and the opportunity to remember and celebrate the love shared.

4. **Inspiration:** A eulogy inspires others to embrace love, nurture relationships, and pursue their passions. It serves as a reminder of the importance of love in shaping a meaningful and fulfilling life.

5. **Unification:** A eulogy brings people together, fostering a sense of unity and shared appreciation for the love the deceased had for people and things. It strengthens relationships and creates a supportive community.

Techniques of a Eulogy that Celebrates Love for People and Things.

1. **Personal anecdotes:** Share memorable stories and experiences that highlight the positive qualities and impact of the person or thing being remembered.

2. **Descriptive language:** Use vivid and heartfelt descriptions to paint a picture of the person or thing, capturing their essence and the emotions they evoked.

3. **Reflection:** Offer personal reflections on the lessons learned or how the person or thing made a difference in your life or the lives of others.

4. **Gratitude:** Express gratitude for the time and experiences shared, acknowledging the value they brought and the lasting impact they had.

5. **Celebration:** Emphasize the joy and positivity associated with the person or thing's presence, celebrating their accomplishments, passions, and the love they cultivated.

Factors of a Eulogy that Celebrates Love for People and Things.

1. **Impact:** Discuss how the person or thing positively influenced others, whether through their actions, relationships, or contributions to a particular field or cause.

2. **Character:** Highlight the admirable qualities and characteristics of the person or thing, such as kindness, resilience, creativity, or dedication.

3. **Relationships:** Recognize the meaningful connections the person or thing had with friends, family, or the community, emphasizing the love and bonds they fostered.

4. **Legacy:** Explore the lasting impact the person or thing leaves behind, considering how they continue to inspire and influence others.

5. **Growth and transformation:** Discuss how the person or thing evolved and grew over time, overcoming challenges and leaving a positive mark on their surroundings.

Causes of a Eulogy that Celebrates Love for People and Things.

1. **Love and compassion:** Emphasize the person or thing's capacity to love and show kindness, highlighting their ability to bring people together and create meaningful connections.

2. **Inspiration:** Discuss how the person or thing served as an inspiration to others, whether through their achievements, creativity, or the values they embodied.

3. **Change and progress:** Highlight the person or thing's contributions to positive change, whether in their personal lives, the community, or a specific field.

4. **Joy and happiness:** Reflect on the joy and happiness the person or thing brought into the lives of others, sharing moments of laughter, shared experiences, and fond memories.

5. **Connection and belonging:** Celebrate the person or thing's ability to create a sense of belonging and foster a supportive

community, emphasizing the importance of human connection.

Importance of a Eulogy that Celebrates Love for People and Things.

1. **Significance:** Emphasize the profound impact the person or thing had on the lives of others, expressing how they were cherished and held in high regard.
2. **Inspiration:** Discuss how the person or thing served as a source of inspiration, motivating others to pursue their passions, overcome challenges, or live more fulfilling lives.
3. **Connection:** Highlight the deep connections and relationships that were formed through the person or thing, emphasizing the bonds of love, friendship, and community they fostered.
4. **Legacy:** Reflect on the lasting legacy the person or thing leaves behind, considering their contributions, achievements, and the positive influence they had on future generations.
5. **Belonging:** Acknowledge the sense of belonging and inclusion that the person or thing provided, creating a space where individuals feel accepted, valued, and loved.

Qualities of a Eulogy that Celebrates Love for People and Things.

1. **Kindness:** Highlight the person or thing's genuine kindness and compassion, focusing on their ability to bring warmth and care into the lives of others.
2. **Resilience:** Celebrate the person or thing's strength and perseverance, noting their ability to overcome challenges and inspire others to face adversity with courage.
3. **Generosity:** Recognize the person or thing's selflessness and generosity, whether through their acts of giving, support, or the time and attention they devoted to others.
4. **Empathy:** Emphasize the person or thing's capacity for empathy and understanding, acknowledging their ability to listen, provide comfort, and offer support during difficult times.
5. **Authenticity:** Celebrate the person or thing's authenticity and genuineness, noting their ability to be true to themselves and inspire others to do the same.

Framework of a Eulogy that Celebrates Love for People and Things.

1. **Introduction:** Begin by setting the stage, providing context, and acknowledging the purpose of the eulogy.
2. **Personal anecdotes:** Share specific stories and memories that illustrate the importance, qualities, and impact of the person or thing being honored.

3. **Reflection and tribute:** Reflect on the significance of the person or thing's presence in your life or the lives of others, paying tribute to their unique qualities and the love they brought.
4. **Commemoration:** Discuss the accomplishments, contributions, and milestones that highlight the person or thing's journey and impact, celebrating their achievements.
5. **Conclusion:** End the eulogy by expressing gratitude for the person or thing's presence, highlighting the enduring love and memories that will continue to be cherished.

Advantages of a Eulogy that Celebrates Love for People and Things.

1. **Inspiration:** Highlight how the person or thing served as a source of inspiration, motivating others to pursue their dreams, overcome obstacles, and live a more fulfilling life.
2. **Love and Support:** Emphasize the love and support that the person or thing provides, creating a sense of security, comfort, and belonging for those around them.
3. **Growth and Learning:** Discuss how the person or thing encouraged personal growth and learning, offering guidance, wisdom, and opportunities for self-improvement.
4. **Joy and Happiness:** Celebrate the joy and happiness that the person or thing brought into the lives of others, creating fond memories and moments of laughter.

5. **Impact and Influence:** Recognize the positive impact and influence the person or thing had on individuals, communities, or a particular field, leaving a lasting legacy.

Disadvantages of a Eulogy that Celebrates Love for People and Things.

1. **Loss and Grief:** Acknowledge the pain and grief associated with the absence of the person or thing, highlighting the void they leave behind and the emotions that come with it.
2. **Dependence:** Discuss any tendencies of dependence that may have developed, where the person or thing became relied upon or indispensable, making their absence more challenging.
3. **Vulnerability:** Recognize the vulnerability that may have arisen when deeply connected to the person or thing, as the potential for heartbreak or disappointment becomes more profound.
4. **Change and Transition:** Address the difficulty of navigating change and transition when the person or thing is no longer present, as it can be unsettling and require adjustment.
5. **Impermanence:** Reflect on the transient nature of life and the realization that all things, including cherished people or things, eventually come to an end.

Chapter 9: A Strong Eulogy.

Giving Your Story Momentum as Protagonists.

A eulogy serves as a powerful tribute, honoring the lives of individuals and things that have impacted us deeply. It provides an opportunity to reflect on their significance, celebrate their achievements, and share their stories. A strong eulogy goes beyond simply recounting memories; it infuses the narrative with momentum, casting the honoree as the protagonist of their own unique and impactful journey. This essay explores the importance of a strong eulogy in giving the story momentum and highlights key elements that contribute to its effectiveness.

1. Setting the Stage: Establishing Context.

To give a eulogy momentum, it is crucial to set the stage by providing context. This includes introducing the honoree, their life experiences, and the impact they had on others. By presenting a clear backdrop, the eulogy gains a foundation upon which the narrative can build.

2. Unveiling the Protagonist: Celebrating Individuality.

A strong eulogy recognizes the honoree as the protagonist of their own story. It celebrates their individuality, unique qualities, and accomplishments. By highlighting their strengths, passions, and contributions, the eulogy weaves a compelling narrative that propels the story forward.

3. Plot Development: Sharing Meaningful Anecdotes.

To give the eulogy momentum, it is essential to share meaningful anecdotes that reflect the honoree's journey. These anecdotes should capture significant moments, experiences, and relationships that shaped their life. By weaving together these stories, the eulogy creates a dynamic narrative arc, engaging the audience and driving the story forward.

4. Conflict and Resolution: Overcoming Challenges.

A strong eulogy acknowledges the challenges the honorees faced and the obstacles they overcame. By highlighting their resilience, determination, and ability to navigate hardships, the eulogy adds depth and momentum to the narrative. It demonstrates the honoree's capacity for growth and inspires others to face adversity with courage.

5. Supporting Characters: Recognizing Relationships.

No story is complete without supporting characters. In a eulogy, it is important to recognize the relationships that were integral to the honoree's life. By acknowledging the love, support, and connections they shared with others, the eulogy adds richness and dimension to the narrative, further fueling its momentum.

6. Themes and Lessons: Reflecting on Impact.

A strong eulogy delves into the themes and lessons that define the honoree's life. It reflects on the impact they had on others, whether through their actions, words, or values. By exploring these themes and imparting the honoree's wisdom, the eulogy inspires the audience and propels the narrative forward with purpose.

7. Climax and Resolution: Celebrating Legacy.

A powerful eulogy builds towards a climax, culminating in a celebration of the honoree's legacy. It encapsulates their enduring impact, the lives they touched, and the contributions they made. By honoring their legacy, the eulogy gives the story a sense of resolution, leaving the audience with a lasting impression and a call to carry forward the honoree's values and achievements.

Tips of Giving Your Story Momentum as Protagonists.

1. **Personalize the Narrative:** Tailor the eulogy to the honoree's unique qualities, experiences, and achievements. By personalizing the narrative, you create a more engaging and heartfelt tribute that resonates with the audience.

2. **Use Vivid Language:** Employ descriptive and evocative language to paint a vivid picture of the honoree's life and impact. This helps to captivate the audience's attention and bring the story to life.

3. **Share Meaningful Anecdotes:** Select anecdotes that capture significant moments or qualities that define the honoree. These anecdotes should be relatable and memorable, allowing the audience to connect with the story on a deeper level.

4. **Include Reflection and Lessons Learned:** Take the opportunity to reflect on the lessons learned from the honoree's life and incorporate them into the eulogy. This adds depth and meaning to the narrative, inspiring others to carry forward the honoree's values and wisdom.

5. **Practice and Rehearse:** Prepare the eulogy in advance and practice delivering it. Rehearsing allows you to become more comfortable with the material, ensuring a smoother delivery during the actual eulogy.

Benefits of Giving Your Story Momentum as Protagonists.

1. **Honoring the Honoree:** A strong eulogy provides a meaningful and dignified tribute to the honoree, celebrating their life, achievements, and impact. It ensures that their memory is honored and cherished.

2. **Emotional Connection:** A well-crafted eulogy has the power to evoke emotions and create a deep emotional

connection with the audience. It allows them to reflect, remember, and celebrate the honoree's life alongside you.

1. **Healing and Closure:** Delivering a strong eulogy can help facilitate the healing process for both the speaker and the audience. It provides an opportunity to express and process grief and find closure in the celebration of the honoree's life.

2. **Inspiration and Motivation:** A powerful eulogy can inspire and motivate others by highlighting the honoree's accomplishments, resilience, and positive qualities. It encourages the audience to embrace their own lives with renewed purpose and determination.

3. **Strengthening Bonds:** The act of delivering a eulogy brings people together in remembrance and celebration. It strengthens bonds within the community, fostering a sense of unity and shared experience.

Functions of Giving Your Story Momentum as Protagonists.

1. **Commemoration:** A eulogy serves as a commemoration of the honoree's life, highlighting their achievements, impact, and the legacy they leave behind.

2. **Storytelling:** A eulogy tells the story of the honoree's life, capturing their experiences, relationships, and personal growth. It serves as a narrative that engages and connects the audience.

3. **Reflection and Remembrance:** A eulogy allows for reflection and remembrance of the honoree's life, providing an opportunity for the audience to recall their memories and experiences with the person being honored.

4. **Uniting the Audience:** A eulogy brings together family, friends, and community members, fostering a sense of unity and shared support as they collectively remember and celebrate the honoree.

5. **Legacy Preservation:** By recounting the honoree's accomplishments and impact, a eulogy helps preserve their legacy. It ensures that their influence and contributions are remembered and passed on to future generations.

Techniques of Giving Your Story Momentum as Protagonists.

1. **Engaging Opening:** Begin the eulogy with a captivating and engaging opening. This can be a heartfelt quote, a personal anecdote, or a thought-provoking question that immediately captures the attention of the audience and sets the tone for the eulogy.

2. **Structured Organization:** Organize the eulogy in a clear and logical structure. This can be chronological, thematic, or a combination of both. A well-structured eulogy allows for a smooth flow of ideas, enabling the audience to follow the narrative easily.

3. **Varied Tone and Pace:** Employ a varied tone and pace throughout the eulogy to maintain the audience's interest. This can include moments of reflection, humor, and emotion.

Changing the tempo and tone helps to create a dynamic and engaging speech.

4. **Use of Visual Aids:** Incorporate visual aids such as photographs, videos, or props to enhance the storytelling experience. Visuals can evoke emotions, make memories come alive, and provide a deeper connection between the audience and the honoree.

5. **Authentic Delivery:** Deliver the eulogy with authenticity, allowing your genuine emotions to shine through. Speak from the heart, maintain eye contact with the audience, and use natural gestures to convey your message. An authentic delivery helps to establish a strong connection with the listeners.

Factors of Giving Your Story Momentum as Protagonists.

1. **Emotional Connection:** Establish an emotional connection with the audience by sharing personal stories, memories, and experiences. Touching on the honoree's impact on people's lives and expressing genuine emotions helps to create a powerful bond between the audience and the narrative.

2. **Relevance to the Audience:** Consider the audience's relationship with the honoree and tailor the eulogy accordingly. Acknowledge their shared experiences, memories, and emotions, ensuring that the eulogy resonates with their connection to the person being honored.

3. **Cultural and Religious Considerations:** Take into account the cultural and religious background of both the honoree and

the audience. Respect any customs, traditions, or beliefs that may influence the eulogy's content and delivery, ensuring that it is sensitive and inclusive.

4. **Time and Context:** Consider the time and context in which the eulogy is being delivered. Adapt the length, tone, and content of the eulogy to suit the occasion, whether it is a formal funeral service or a more informal gathering of friends and family.

5. **Personal Connection to the Honoree:** Reflect on your connection to the honoree and let it guide your storytelling. Sharing your own experiences, perspectives, and insights adds depth and authenticity to the eulogy, making it more meaningful for both you and the audience.

Causes of Giving Your Story Momentum as Protagonists.

1. **Love and Affection:** The primary cause of a strong eulogy is the deep love and affection felt for the honoree. Genuine care and admiration for the person being honored drive the desire to deliver a heartfelt tribute that does justice to their memory.

2. **Impact and Influence:** The honoree's impact and influence on your life and the lives of others serve as a cause for delivering a strong eulogy. Recognizing their significance and the positive changes they brought about motivates you to share their story with passion and momentum.

3. **Gratitude and Appreciation:** A strong eulogy is often caused by a deep sense of gratitude and appreciation for the honoree's presence in your life. Expressing this gratitude

through a well-crafted eulogy becomes a way to honor their memory and the impact they had on you.

4. **Sense of Duty:** The responsibility and duty felt to properly honor the honoree's life and legacy can be a cause for delivering a strong eulogy. Recognizing the importance of the occasion and the role you play in commemorating their memory motivates you to give your best effort in delivering a powerful tribute.

5. **Celebration of Life:** Ultimately, the cause behind a strong eulogy is the desire to celebrate the honoree's life. Focusing on their accomplishments, cherished memories, and positive qualities allows you to create a eulogy that honors their legacy and gives their story the momentum it deserves.

Importance of Giving Your Story Momentum as Protagonists.

1. **Honoring the Honoree:** A strong eulogy is important because it provides a meaningful and dignified tribute to the honoree. It allows their life, accomplishments, and impact to be acknowledged and celebrated.

2. **Emotional Connection:** A well-crafted eulogy creates an emotional connection between the audience and the honoree. It allows people to reflect, remember, and pay their respects, fostering a sense of unity and support.

3. **Preserving Legacy:** A eulogy is an opportunity to preserve the honoree's legacy. By sharing their stories, achievements, and values, the eulogy ensures that their memory continues to inspire and influence future generations.

4. **Healing and Closure:** Delivering a strong eulogy can facilitate the healing process for both the speaker and the audience. It provides a platform to express and process grief, find closure, and move forward with a sense of peace.

5. **Inspiration and Reflection:** A powerful eulogy can inspire and motivate others. It prompts the audience to reflect on their own lives, values, and relationships, encouraging them to live with purpose and make a positive impact.

Qualities of Giving Your Story Momentum as Protagonists.

1. **Authenticity:** A strong eulogy is authentic, reflecting the genuine emotions and experiences of the speaker. It is sincere, heartfelt, and true to the honoree's character.

2. **Respectful:** A eulogy should be respectful of the honoree's life, beliefs, and values. It should avoid judgment or criticism, focusing instead on honoring their achievements and contributions.

3. **Coherence:** A well-crafted eulogy is coherent, with ideas flowing logically and smoothly. It maintains a clear structure and connects different aspects of the honoree's life and impact.

4. **Engaging:** An effective eulogy captures the audience's attention and keeps them engaged throughout. It uses storytelling techniques, anecdotes, and personal connections to create a compelling narrative.

5. **Inspiring:** A strong eulogy inspires and uplifts the audience. It highlights the honoree's positive qualities, achievements,

and impact, motivating others to live with similar values and make a difference in their own lives.

Framework of Giving Your Story Momentum as Protagonists.

1. **Introduction:** Begin with an engaging opening, setting the stage for the eulogy and capturing the audience's attention.

2. **Personal Stories and Anecdotes:** Share meaningful personal stories and anecdotes that highlight the honoree's life, values, and impact. These stories should be relatable and resonate with the audience.

3. **Reflection and Lessons:** Reflect on the lessons learned from the honoree's life and incorporate them into the eulogy. Share insights and wisdom gained from their experiences, allowing the audience to learn and grow.

4. **Acknowledge Relationships and Support:** Recognize the important relationships and support systems in the honoree's life. Express gratitude for the love and care they received and the impact these relationships had on their journey.

5. **Conclusion:** End the eulogy with a heartfelt conclusion that celebrates the honoree's legacy and leaves the audience with a lasting impression. Provide a call to action, encouraging listeners to carry forward the honoree's values and make a positive impact in their own lives.

Advantages of Giving Your Story Momentum as Protagonists.

1. **Honoring the Honoree:** A strong eulogy allows you to honor the honoree's life, accomplishments, and impact. It provides a heartfelt tribute that celebrates their memory and pays respects to their legacy.

2. **Emotional Connection:** A well-crafted eulogy creates an emotional connection with the audience. It allows them to reflect, remember, and share in the collective grief and celebration of the honoree's life.

3. **Healing and Closure:** Delivering a strong eulogy can facilitate healing and closure for both the speaker and the listeners. It provides an opportunity to express and process grief, find solace, and move forward in the grieving process.

4. **Inspiration and Motivation:** A powerful eulogy can inspire and motivate others. It highlights the honoree's achievements, values, and impact, encouraging listeners to live with purpose, make positive changes, and cherish their relationships.

5. **Strengthening Bonds:** Delivering a strong eulogy brings people together in remembrance and celebration. It strengthens bonds within the community, fostering a sense of unity, support, and shared memories.

Disadvantages of Giving Your Story Momentum as Protagonists.

1. **Emotional Strain:** Delivering a eulogy can be emotionally challenging, especially if you have a close relationship with

the honoree. It may be difficult to maintain composure while speaking about their life and the impact of their loss.

2. **Pressure to Perform:** There can be pressure to deliver a strong eulogy, as it is a significant responsibility and a highly observed moment during the memorial service. The fear of not meeting expectations can add stress and anxiety.

3. **Time Constraints:** Eulogies are typically delivered within a limited time frame, which can make it challenging to cover all aspects of the honoree's life and impact. Choosing what to include and what to omit can be a difficult decision.

4. **Audience Expectations:** Different audience members may have varying expectations of what a eulogy should entail. Balancing the desires of family members, friends, and cultural traditions can be challenging and may lead to conflicting expectations.

5. **Vulnerability and Emotional Exposure:** Delivering a eulogy requires vulnerability and emotional exposure. Sharing personal stories and emotions in front of a large audience can be intimidating and may leave you feeling emotionally drained.

Chapter 10: Drafting the Eulogy.

Celebrating the Life of a Protagonist.

A eulogy is a profound way to honor and remember the life of a person who has passed away. It allows us to reflect on their journey, achievements, and impact on the world. In this essay, we will explore the unique concept of drafting a eulogy as a protagonist, envisioning the life of an individual as a story with themselves as the central character. By adopting this perspective, we can celebrate the virtues, accomplishments, and personal growth of the departed individual from a narrative standpoint.

1. Setting the Stage.

- Introduce the protagonist's name and background.
- Describe the setting in which their life unfolded.
- Highlight significant events or milestones that shaped their journey.
- Establish the central theme of the eulogy.

2. The Call to Adventure.

- Discuss the protagonist's initial challenges and obstacles.
- Explore their motivations and aspirations.
- Detail the moment that set them on their unique path.
- Emphasize their courage to embark on a transformative journey.

3. Rising Action and Character Development.

- Narrate the protagonist's progressive growth and development.
- Highlight key experiences, relationships, and lessons learned.
- Discuss their triumphs and setbacks, and how they overcame adversity.
- Showcase their evolving beliefs, values, and ideals.

4. Climax and Legacy.

- Describe the pinnacle of the protagonist's life, their greatest achievement, or the moment of profound impact.
- Discuss the legacy they leave behind and how it will continue to inspire others.
- Reflect on the protagonist's transformation and growth.
- Emphasize their lasting contribution to their community or society.

5. Falling Action and Resolution.

- Discuss the protagonist's later years and how they gracefully navigated the challenges of aging.
- Highlight their continued pursuit of knowledge, wisdom, or personal fulfillment.
- Describe their relationships and their profound effect on others.
- Acknowledge any regrets or unfinished dreams, if applicable.

6. The Denouement.

- Summarize the protagonist's life journey and the impact they had on the world.
- Express gratitude for their presence and the lessons they taught us.
- Offer words of comfort and solace to the grieving audience.
- Conclude with a call to action, encouraging others to embrace their heroic journeys.

Tips for drafting the eulogy.

1. **Reflect on their journey:** Start by reflecting on the protagonist's life journey, highlighting key moments, challenges, and achievements that defined their character.
2. **Capture their essence:** Focus on capturing the essence of the protagonist's personality, values, and impact on others. Share anecdotes, stories, and examples that showcase their unique qualities.

3. **Include personal touch:** Incorporate personal memories and experiences you shared with the protagonist, demonstrating the depth of your relationship and the impact they had on your life.

4. **Balance humor and emotion:** Strike a balance between sharing heartfelt emotions and incorporating moments of levity. Mix touching stories with humorous anecdotes to create a well-rounded tribute that reflects their multifaceted nature.

5. **Keep it concise:** While it's important to honor the protagonist's life, it's also crucial to keep the eulogy concise. Focus on the most significant aspects and keep it within a reasonable time frame to ensure the audience remains engaged.

Benefits of drafting a eulogy.

1. **Honoring their legacy:** Writing a eulogy allows you to honor the protagonist's legacy by acknowledging their accomplishments, impact, and the lasting impression they left on others.

2. **Emotional release:** Expressing your thoughts and emotions through a eulogy can provide a cathartic experience, helping you cope with grief and find closure.

3. **Bringing comfort to others:** A well-crafted eulogy can offer solace and comfort to those mourning the loss, providing an opportunity to remember and celebrate the protagonist's life together.

4. **Preserving memories:** By documenting the protagonist's life in a eulogy, you contribute to preserving their memories for future generations, ensuring their story lives on.

5. **Strengthening bonds:** Sharing a eulogy at a funeral or memorial service brings people together, fostering a sense of community and unity as they collectively remember and honor the protagonist.

Functions of a eulogy.

1. **Commemoration:** A eulogy serves as a commemoration of the protagonist's life, acknowledging their achievements, experiences, and the impact they had on others.

2. **Reflection:** It allows mourners to reflect on the protagonist's life, highlighting the lessons learned, the inspiration they provided, and the values they upheld.

3. **Emotional connection:** A eulogy helps establish an emotional connection between the audience and the protagonist, evoking feelings of love, gratitude, and nostalgia.

4. **Healing and closure:** Delivering or listening to a eulogy can facilitate the healing process, providing a sense of closure and allowing mourners to say goodbye in a meaningful way.

5. **Celebration of life:** Ultimately, a eulogy functions as a celebration of the protagonist's life, focusing on their positive contributions, memorable moments, and the legacy they leave behind.

Techniques for drafting the eulogy.

1. **Storytelling:** Use storytelling techniques to engage the audience and paint a vivid picture of the protagonist's life, emphasizing key moments, relationships, and accomplishments.

2. **Personalization:** Incorporate personal anecdotes, memories, and reflections to create a heartfelt and authentic tribute that captures the essence of the protagonist.

3. **Structure and organization:** Use a clear structure and logical flow to guide the eulogy, ensuring that it is easy to follow and delivers a cohesive narrative.

4. **Emotional appeal:** Employ emotional language and heartfelt expressions to evoke a range of emotions in the audience, allowing them to connect with the protagonist's life and impact.

5. **Vivid language and imagery:** Utilize descriptive and evocative language, along with vivid imagery, to bring the protagonist's experiences and qualities to life, making the eulogy more engaging.

Factors to consider when drafting the eulogy.

1. **Protagonist's personality:** Consider the protagonist's unique personality traits, values, passions, and beliefs, and how these influenced their actions and interactions with others.

2. **Impact on others:** Reflect on how the protagonist touched the lives of others, whether through their relationships, accomplishments, or acts of kindness and generosity.

3. **Life experiences:** Take into account the significant life experiences and milestones of the protagonist, such as their education, career, family life, and any notable achievements or challenges they faced.

4. **Contributions to society:** Consider the protagonist's contributions to their community, profession, or causes they were passionate about, highlighting the positive impact they made on a larger scale.

5. **Legacy and lasting impression:** Reflect on the lasting impression the protagonist leaves behind, including the values they instilled in others, the memories they created, and the lessons they taught.

Courses to take when preparing a eulogy.

1. **Public speaking:** Taking a public speaking course can help improve your delivery, confidence, and ability to engage the audience effectively while delivering the eulogy.

2. **Writing and storytelling:** Enhancing your writing and storytelling skills through courses can help you craft a compelling and impactful eulogy that resonates with the audience.

3. **Grief counseling:** Consider attending a grief counseling course to understand the emotional aspects of loss and grief,

allowing you to approach the eulogy with empathy and sensitivity.

4. **Communication and empathy:** Courses focused on communication and empathy can help you connect with the audience on a deeper level, delivering a eulogy that is both compassionate and relatable.

5. **History or biographical research:** If you require further information about the protagonist's life, considering courses in history or biographical research can assist you in conducting thorough research and gathering relevant details for the eulogy.

Importance of drafting a eulogy.

1. **Tribute and Honor:** Drafting a eulogy allows you to pay tribute and honor the life and accomplishments of the protagonist, acknowledging their significance and impact.

2. **Closure and healing:** Writing a eulogy can provide a sense of closure and facilitate the healing process for both the speaker and the audience, allowing for reflection and emotional release.

3. **Celebration of life:** A eulogy serves as a platform to celebrate the protagonist's life, focusing on their positive qualities, achievements, and the joy they bring to others.

4. **Remembrance and legacy:** By crafting a eulogy, you contribute to preserving the memory and legacy of the protagonist, ensuring that their story lives on in the hearts and minds of those who knew them.

5. **Comfort and support:** Delivering or hearing a eulogy can offer comfort and support to those mourning the loss, providing a space to remember, grieve, and find solace together.

Qualities to emphasize in the eulogy.

1. **Character:** Highlight the protagonist's admirable character traits, such as kindness, resilience, generosity, or compassion, demonstrating the positive impact they had on others.
2. **Achievements:** Celebrate the protagonist's notable accomplishments, whether personal, professional, or in service to others, showcasing their dedication, talent, and contributions.
3. **Relationships:** Emphasize the protagonist's meaningful relationships, illustrating the love, support, and connections they fostered with family, friends, and community.
4. **Values:** Discuss the protagonist's core values and principles, underscoring their integrity, honesty, empathy, or commitment to making a difference.
5. **Impact:** Focus on the protagonist's impact on the lives of others, sharing stories, anecdotes, and testimonials that showcase the ways they influenced and inspired those around them.

Framework for drafting the eulogy.

1. **Introduction:** Begin with a warm and heartfelt introduction, acknowledging the purpose of the eulogy and setting the tone for the tribute.

2. **Personal connection:** Share personal memories, experiences, or anecdotes that highlight your relationship with the protagonist and the impact they had on your life.

3. **Life journey:** Reflect on the key moments, milestones, challenges, and accomplishments that defined the protagonist's life journey, weaving a narrative that captures their essence.

4. **Qualities and values:** Discuss the protagonist's admirable qualities, values, and virtues, emphasizing how these shaped their character and influenced their actions.

5. **Impact and legacy:** Highlight how the protagonist made a difference in the lives of others, whether through their relationships, achievements, or contributions to society.

Advantages of drafting a eulogy.

1. **Honoring the deceased:** Writing a eulogy allows you to honor and pay tribute to the life, accomplishments, and impact of the protagonist, ensuring their memory is cherished and celebrated.

2. **Emotional catharsis:** Drafting a eulogy can provide emotional catharsis for the speaker, offering a platform to express grief, share memories, and find solace in the act of remembering.

3. **Healing and closure:** Delivering or hearing a eulogy can contribute to the healing process, providing a sense of closure and allowing mourners to say goodbye in a meaningful way.

4. **Sharing memories and stories:** Writing a eulogy provides an opportunity to share cherished memories, stories, and anecdotes about the protagonist, fostering a sense of connection and comfort among mourners.

5. **Preserving a legacy:** By documenting the protagonist's life in a eulogy, you contribute to preserving their legacy for future generations, ensuring their story lives on.

Disadvantages of drafting a eulogy.

1. **Emotional difficulty:** Writing and delivering a eulogy can be emotionally challenging, as it requires revisiting memories and emotions associated with the loss of the protagonist.

2. **Time-consuming:** Crafting a thoughtful and meaningful eulogy can be time-consuming, particularly if you want to ensure that it captures the essence of the protagonist's life and impact.

3. **Performance pressure:** Delivering a eulogy in front of an audience can be intimidating and may create performance pressure for the speaker, adding a layer of stress during an already emotional time.

4. **Grief triggers:** Writing or listening to a eulogy can evoke strong emotions and grief triggers, potentially intensifying the mourning process for some individuals.

5. **Limited perspective:** Depending on the relationship with the protagonist, the eulogy may provide a limited perspective of their life, potentially missing certain aspects or viewpoints that others may have experienced or valued.

Chapter 11: The protagonist's medium- and long-term visions.

The protagonist's medium- and long-term visions are centered around personal growth, making a positive impact on society, and pursuing their passions.

In the medium term, the protagonist envisions a journey of self-discovery and personal development. They aspire to acquire new skills, broaden their knowledge, and explore different interests. This could involve pursuing further education, attending workshops or conferences, or engaging in immersive experiences that expand their horizons. By investing in their growth, the protagonist aims to unlock their full potential and gain a deeper understanding of themselves and the world around them.

Aligned with personal growth, the protagonist's vision also includes making a positive impact on society. They seek to contribute to causes they care about, whether it's environmental conservation, social justice, education, or community development. This may involve volunteering, advocacy work, or actively participating in initiatives that address pressing societal issues. By engaging in meaningful actions, the protagonist aims to create positive change and leave a lasting impact on the lives of others.

Looking towards the long term, the protagonist's vision involves aligning their career with their passions and values. They strive to find work that is fulfilling, purpose-driven and allows them to make a meaningful contribution to society. This could mean pursuing a career in a field they are passionate about, starting their venture to address a specific problem, or working in an organization that aligns with their values. The protagonist envisions a future where their work becomes a source of personal satisfaction and a means to create a positive ripple effect in the world.

Furthermore, the long-term vision includes fostering meaningful relationships and connections. The protagonist recognizes the importance of building strong bonds with family, friends, and like-minded individuals who share their values and aspirations. They envision a supportive network that encourages collaboration, learning, and personal growth. These relationships will not only provide the protagonist with emotional support but also offer opportunities for collaboration and collective action toward shared goals.

Protagonist's Medium- and Long-Term Visions.

- **Personal Growth:** The protagonist envisions continuous self-improvement and acquiring new skills, knowledge, and experiences.
- **Impactful Contribution:** The protagonist aspires to make a positive difference in society and contribute to causes they care about.
- **Passion Pursuit:** The protagonist seeks to align their career and activities with their passions and interests.
- **Meaningful Relationships:** The protagonist values building strong connections and fostering supportive relationships with like-minded individuals.
- **Legacy Building:** The protagonist aims to leave a lasting impact and create a meaningful legacy through their actions.

Tips for Achieving the Visions.

1. **Set Clear Goals:** Define specific, measurable, achievable, relevant, and time-bound (SMART) goals related to personal growth, impact, passion pursuit, relationships, and legacy building.
2. **Embrace Continuous Learning:** Cultivate a growth mindset and actively seek opportunities for learning and self-improvement, such as attending workshops, reading books, or taking courses.
3. **Take Action:** Break down long-term visions into actionable steps and consistently work towards them, overcoming obstacles and persevering through challenges.

4. **Seek Guidance and Support:** Surround yourself with mentors, coaches, and a supportive network that can provide guidance, accountability, and encouragement along your journey.

5. **Reflect and Adjust:** Regularly assess your progress, reflect on your experiences, and adjust your plans as needed to stay aligned with your visions.

Benefits of Pursuing These Visions.

1. **Personal Fulfillment:** Working towards personal growth, making an impact, pursuing passions, and building meaningful relationships can lead to a deep sense of fulfillment and satisfaction.

2. **Increased Resilience:** Embracing challenges and overcoming obstacles in pursuit of long-term visions can cultivate resilience and strengthen one's ability to adapt and persevere.

3. **Greater Purpose and Meaning:** Having a clear vision and working towards it can provide a sense of purpose and meaning in life, enhancing overall well-being.

4. **Positive Impact on Others:** Making a difference and contributing to causes can inspire and positively influence others, creating a ripple effect of change.

5. **Legacy and Recognition:** By leaving a lasting impact and building a meaningful legacy, the protagonist can be recognized for their contributions and leave a positive mark on the world.

Functions Associated with the Visions.

1. **Motivational Driver:** The visions serve as a motivation for the protagonist to take action, overcome challenges, and stay committed to their goals.

2. **Directional Guide:** The visions provide a sense of direction and purpose, helping the protagonist make decisions and prioritize their actions.

3. **Self-Reflection Tool:** Reviewing progress towards the visions allows the protagonist to reflect on their growth, achievements, and areas for improvement.

4. **Connection Builder:** Pursuing the visions can help the protagonist connect with like-minded individuals, organizations, and communities who share similar values and goals.

5. **Life Enrichment:** Working towards the visions can bring fulfillment, satisfaction, and a sense of fulfillment, enhancing the overall quality of life.

Techniques to Support the Visions.

1. **Goal Setting:** The protagonist sets specific, measurable, achievable, relevant, and time-bound (SMART) goals to guide their progress and keep them accountable.

2. **Continuous Learning:** The protagonist embraces lifelong learning through reading, attending workshops, taking courses, and seeking new experiences.

3. **Self-Reflection:** Regular self-reflection helps the protagonist assess their growth, strengths, weaknesses, and areas for improvement.

4. **Networking and Collaboration:** The protagonist actively engages in networking and seeks opportunities to collaborate with individuals who share similar visions and goals.

5. **Action Planning:** The protagonist breaks down their visions into actionable steps and creates detailed plans to move forward and achieve their desired outcomes.

Factors Influencing the Visions.

1. **Personal Values:** The protagonist's core values play a significant role in shaping their visions and determining the causes and areas they want to impact.

2. **Life Experiences:** Past experiences, both positive and negative, can shape the protagonist's visions by influencing their worldview, passions, and desires for change.

3. **External Influences:** Society, culture, family, and mentors can impact the protagonist's visions by providing guidance, inspiration, or exposure to certain causes.

4. **Personal Motivation:** The protagonist's inner drive, aspirations, and desires for personal growth and impact motivate and influence their visions.

5. **Global Challenges:** The protagonist's visions may be influenced by pressing global challenges such as climate change, inequality, or social justice issues, driving them to make a difference in these areas.

Causes Supported by the Visions.

1. **Environmental Conservation:** The protagonist may be driven to address environmental issues such as climate change, deforestation, or pollution.

2. **Education and Empowerment:** The protagonist may aim to improve access to education, promote lifelong learning, and empower individuals for personal and societal growth.

3. **Social Justice and Equality:** The protagonist may seek to address social inequalities, fight against discrimination, and advocate for justice and equality for all.

4. **Health and Well-being:** The protagonist maybe passionate about promoting physical and mental health, improving access to healthcare, and fostering well-being in communities.

5. **Community Development:** The protagonist may focus on uplifting communities, improving infrastructure, supporting local economies, and creating sustainable development opportunities.

Important Aspects for Achieving the Visions.

1. **Self-Awareness:** The protagonist recognizes their strengths, weaknesses, values, and passions, which guide their personal growth and contribution.

2. **Goal Alignment:** The protagonist ensures that their visions and goals are aligned with their values, passions, and overall life purpose.

3. **Resilience:** The protagonist develops resilience to overcome obstacles, setbacks, and challenges encountered on their journey toward their visions.

4. **Continuous Learning:** The protagonist embraces lifelong learning to acquire new skills, knowledge, and insights that support their visions.

5. **Adaptability:** The protagonist remains open to change, adapts to new circumstances, and adjusts their strategies as needed to stay on track with their visions.

Qualities to Support the Visions.

1. **Determination:** The protagonist demonstrates persistence, perseverance, and a strong drive to pursue their visions despite obstacles.

2. **Empathy:** The protagonist possesses empathy, compassion, and a genuine concern for the well-being of others, which fuels their impactful contribution.

3. **Integrity:** The protagonist upholds ethical standards, acts with honesty and transparency, and maintains consistency between their values and actions.

4. **Collaboration:** The protagonist values teamwork, actively seeks collaboration and engages in collective efforts to achieve their vision.

5. **Visionary Thinking:** The protagonist possesses the ability to think creatively, envision possibilities, and see the bigger picture in pursuit of their visions.

Frameworks to Guide the Visions.

1. **Personal Development Frameworks:** The protagonist utilizes frameworks like the "Growth Mindset," "SMART Goals," or "SWOT Analysis" to structure their growth journey.

2. **Social Impact Frameworks:** The protagonist adopts frameworks such as the "Theory of Change," "Impact Measurement and Evaluation," or "Design Thinking" to maximize their contribution and assess their impact on societal issues.

3. **Values Alignment Frameworks:** The protagonist employs frameworks like "Values Clarification," "Ethical Decision Making," or "Ikigai" to ensure their visions and actions align with their core values.

4. **Relationship Building Frameworks:** The protagonist utilizes frameworks like "Active Listening," "Empathy Mapping," or "Nonviolent Communication" to foster meaningful relationships and effective communication.

5. **Legacy Planning Frameworks:** The protagonist employs frameworks such as "Personal Legacy Statement," "Social Impact Assessment," or "Long-Term Goals Setting" to plan and create a lasting legacy aligned with their visions.

Advantages of the protagonist's medium- and long-term visions.

1. **Clarity of direction:** Having clear visions helps the protagonist stay focused and motivated, providing a sense of purpose and guiding their actions.

2. **Strategic planning:** Medium- and long-term visions enable the protagonist to develop strategic plans, identify milestones, and allocate resources effectively.

3. **Innovation and growth:** Visions encourage the protagonist to think creatively, explore new ideas, and pursue innovative solutions, fostering personal and professional growth.

4. **Alignment and collaboration:** Visions can inspire and rally others around a common goal, fostering collaboration and creating a shared sense of purpose within teams or organizations.

5. **Resilience and perseverance:** Having long-term visions helps the protagonist stay resilient in the face of challenges, setbacks, or temporary failures, as they can see beyond immediate obstacles.

Disadvantages of the protagonist's medium- and long-term visions.

1. **Rigidity:** Overly rigid visions may limit the protagonist's ability to adapt to changing circumstances or take advantage of unforeseen opportunities.

2. **Unrealistic expectations:** If visions are overly ambitious or unrealistic, they can lead to disappointment and frustration if not achieved, potentially demotivating the protagonist.

3. **Tunnel vision:** Focusing solely on long-term visions may cause the protagonist to overlook important short-term goals or immediate priorities.

4. **Lack of flexibility:** Strict adherence to long-term visions may prevent the protagonist from being open to alternative paths or adjusting course when necessary.

5. **Potential burnout:** Pursuing ambitious visions without considering personal well-being or work-life balance may lead to burnout or excessive stress over time.

Chapter 12: A Protagonist's Journey.

Completing Tasks and Unveiling Destiny.

The concept of a protagonist completing tasks lies at the heart of countless narratives across various mediums. From ancient myths to modern novels, movies, and video games, the journey of a hero or heroine embarking on a series of tasks is a timeless narrative structure. These tasks, often demanding and perilous, propel the protagonist forward, shaping their character, revealing their strengths and weaknesses, and ultimately leading them towards their destined fate. In this chapter we'll explore the significance and implications of a protagonist completing tasks, delving into the transformative nature of these challenges and the profound impact they have on the character's development.

1. The Role of Tasks in Character Development.

- **Establishing the Hero's Journey.**
- The monomyth and Joseph Campbell's archetypal hero's journey.

- The call to adventure and the protagonist's initial resistance.
- Crossing the threshold and embracing the journey.
- **The Transformational Power of Tasks.**
- Challenges as catalysts for growth and change.
- Testing the protagonist's skills, resilience, and determination.
- Overcoming obstacles and acquiring new abilities.
- Inner conflicts and the hero's moral development.
- **Task-Based Narratives Across Different Mediums.**
- **Classical examples:** Hercules, Odysseus, and Gilgamesh.
- **Contemporary examples:** Harry Potter, Frodo Baggins, and Katniss Everdeen.
- Task-based video games and interactive storytelling.

2. The Quest for Purpose and Destiny.

- **Protagonists as Agents of Change.**
- The protagonist's quest to fulfill a higher purpose.
- The burden of responsibility and the weight of destiny.
- Inspiring hope and motivating others.
- **Symbolism and Allegory in Task Completion.**
- Tasks as metaphors for life's challenges and personal growth.
- Archetypal symbolism in task-based narratives.
- The hero's journey is a metaphor for the human experience.
- **The Balance of Fate and Free Will.**
- Struggling against predetermined paths.
- The intersection of choice and destiny.
- The consequences of task completion and the unfolding of fate.

3. Lessons and Reflections on Task Completion.

- **Resilience, Determination, and Perseverance.**
- The importance of resilience in the face of adversity.
- Learning from failure and embracing setbacks.
- The power of determination and unwavering resolve.
- **Self-Discovery and Identity Formation.**
- Exploring one's true self through the completion of tasks.
- Unveiling hidden strengths and confronting weaknesses.
- Identity formation through task-based challenges.

- **Empathy, Compassion, and the Hero's Journey.**
- Understanding the struggles of others through shared challenges.
- Cultivating empathy and compassion through task completion.
- The hero's journey is a call to action for societal change.

Tips for a protagonist's journey of completing tasks and unveiling destiny.

1. **Define Clear Goals:** Start by defining clear and specific goals for your protagonist. This helps provide direction and purpose to their journey, making it easier to identify the tasks they need to complete.

2. **Break Tasks into Smaller Steps:** Complex tasks can often be overwhelming. Encourage your protagonist to break them

down into smaller, manageable steps. This allows them to focus on one task at a time, making their journey more achievable and less daunting.

3. **Embrace Challenges and Adversity:** Challenges and adversity are inevitable on a protagonist's journey. Encourage your protagonist to embrace these obstacles as opportunities for growth and development. Overcoming challenges builds character and adds depth to the narrative.

4. **Seek Guidance and Support:** Your protagonist doesn't have to face their journey alone. Encourage them to seek guidance and support from mentors, allies, or friends. These relationships can provide valuable insights, advice, and assistance in completing tasks and understanding their destiny.

5. **Reflect and Learn from Experiences:** Throughout the journey, encourage your protagonist to reflect on their experiences and learn from them. Each completed task and obstacle should provide valuable lessons and insights that contribute to their personal growth and the unveiling of their destiny.

Benefits for a protagonist's journey of completing tasks and unveiling destiny.

1. **Personal Growth:** Completing tasks and unveiling destiny allows the protagonist to undergo personal growth, developing new skills, knowledge, and perspectives along the way.

2. **Fulfillment and Satisfaction:** Accomplishing tasks and uncovering one's destiny brings a sense of fulfillment and satisfaction, providing a sense of purpose and meaning to the protagonist's journey.

3. **Story Progression:** Completing tasks drives the story forward, creating momentum and propelling the protagonist toward their ultimate destiny. This keeps the readers engaged and invested in the narrative.

4. **Character Development:** Task completion and the revelation of destiny provide opportunities for deepening the protagonist's character. They can face moral dilemmas, make difficult choices, and evolve as individuals throughout their journey.

5. **Inspiring Others:** A protagonist's journey can inspire and motivate others who relate to their struggles and triumphs. By completing tasks and unveiling their destiny, the protagonist becomes a source of inspiration to others, encouraging them to pursue their own goals.

Functions for a protagonist's journey of completing tasks and unveiling destiny.

1. **Plot Advancement:** Completing tasks and unveiling destiny serve as key plot points, driving the story forward and keeping the readers engaged.

2. **Conflict Resolution:** Tasks often involve overcoming conflicts, and by completing them, the protagonist resolves these conflicts, creating a sense of closure and progress.

3. **Foreshadowing:** Tasks can foreshadow future events or provide clues about the protagonist's destiny, building suspense and anticipation for what's to come.

4. **Character Arc Completion:** Through task completion and unveiling destiny, the protagonist's character arc reaches its culmination, bringing resolution and growth to their journey.

5. **Theme Exploration:** Tasks and the revelation of destiny allow the exploration of themes such as fate, self-discovery, and the power of perseverance, adding depth and complexity to the narrative.

Techniques that can enhance a protagonist's journey of completing tasks and unveiling destiny.

1. **Foreshadowing:** Use subtle hints, symbols, or dialogue early on in the story to foreshadow the tasks the protagonist will need to complete or the destiny they will eventually unveil. This builds anticipation and keeps readers engaged.

2. **Plot Twists:** Incorporate unexpected plot twists that challenge the protagonist's assumptions and force them to adapt their approach to completing tasks and understanding their destiny. This adds excitement and unpredictability to the narrative.

3. **Symbolism:** Utilize symbolic elements throughout the story to represent the protagonist's journey. For example, recurring motifs, objects, or settings can convey deeper meanings and provide insight into the protagonist's progression.

4. **Inner Conflict:** Explore the protagonist's internal struggles and conflicts as they navigate their journey. This could involve conflicting desires, doubts, or moral dilemmas that the protagonist must resolve to complete tasks and grasp their ultimate destiny.

5. **Time Pressure:** Introduce a sense of urgency and time constraints to the protagonist's journey. This creates tension and adds a thrilling element as the protagonist races against time to complete tasks and fulfill their destiny.

Factors of a protagonist's journey to complete tasks and unveiling destiny.

1. **Motivation:** The protagonist's motivation plays a crucial role in driving their journey. It could be a personal goal, a quest for justice, or an inner desire that propels them forward in completing tasks and discovering their destiny.

2. **External Influences:** External factors such as mentors, allies, or adversaries can significantly impact the protagonist's journey. These influences may provide guidance, hinder progress, or present unexpected challenges that shape the protagonist's path.

3. **Past Experiences:** The protagonist's past experiences, traumas, or achievements can influence their approach to tasks and their understanding of their destiny. Their past shapes their present choices and actions, affecting the outcome of their journey.

4. **Environment and Setting:** The environment and setting in which the protagonist operates can have a significant impact on their journey. Whether it's a fantastical world, a post-apocalyptic landscape, or a mundane everyday setting, the surroundings influence the tasks they encounter and their understanding of their destiny.

5. **Beliefs and Values:** The protagonist's personal beliefs, values, and worldview shape their perception of tasks and their destiny. These factors drive their decisions, actions, and the moral dilemmas they face throughout their journey.

Causes for a protagonist's journey of completing tasks and unveiling destiny.

1. **Call to Adventure:** The protagonist's journey is often triggered by a call to adventure, an event or circumstance that sets them on their path. This could be a prophecy, a sudden incident, or a personal revelation that causes them to embark on their quest.

2. **External Conflict:** External conflicts, such as an antagonist or opposing forces, can cause the protagonist to undertake tasks and unravel their destiny. These conflicts propel the story forward and create challenges the protagonist must overcome.

3. **Curiosity and Discovery:** The protagonist's innate curiosity or desire for knowledge can be a cause for embarking on their journey. They may seek answers, unravel mysteries, or

uncover hidden truths, leading them to complete tasks and uncover their destiny.

4. **Personal Growth:** The need for personal growth or self-improvement can motivate the protagonist to undertake tasks and unveil their destiny. They may feel the need to prove themselves, overcome weaknesses, or achieve a higher sense of purpose.

5. **External Obligation:** The protagonist may have external obligations, responsibilities, or duties that drive them to complete tasks and fulfill their destiny. This could be a promise, a duty to protect others, or a quest for redemption.

Importance for a protagonist's journey of completing tasks and unveiling destiny.

1. **Narrative Engagement:** A protagonist's journey of completing tasks and unveiling destiny is essential for capturing and maintaining readers' or viewers' attention. It provides a central storyline that keeps them engaged and invested in the protagonist's development.

2. **Character Development:** This journey allows for significant character development. Through completing tasks and unveiling destiny, the protagonist undergoes personal growth, faces challenges, and evolves as an individual, making them more compelling and relatable to the audience.

3. **Theme Exploration:** The protagonist's journey provides a platform to explore various themes, such as self-discovery, destiny, resilience, and the power of determination. These

themes can resonate with the audience and offer valuable insights and reflections.

4. **Emotional Connection:** A well-crafted protagonist's journey can evoke emotions in the audience, ranging from excitement and anticipation to empathy and inspiration. It creates a strong emotional bond between the audience and the character, making the narrative more impactful.

5. **Reflection on Human Experience:** The protagonist's journey reflects the universal human experience of facing challenges, pursuing goals, and discovering one's purpose. It allows the audience to reflect on their own lives, aspirations, and the transformative power of personal journeys.

Qualities for a protagonist's journey of completing tasks and unveiling destiny.

1. **Relatability:** A protagonist should possess qualities that resonate with the audience, making them relatable and compelling. This could include vulnerabilities, strengths, flaws, or struggles that mirror the experiences of the audience.

2. **Determination:** The protagonist should exhibit a strong sense of determination and resilience. This quality helps them persevere through challenges, overcome obstacles, and remain committed to completing tasks and unveiling their destiny.

3. **Growth Mindset:** A growth mindset is crucial for the protagonist to adapt, learn, and grow throughout their

journey. They should be open to new experiences, willing to learn from failures and embrace change as they progress toward their destiny.

4. **Complexity:** A complex protagonist adds depth and nuance to the narrative. They should possess layered traits, conflicting desires, and internal struggles that create a multidimensional character, capturing the audience's attention and curiosity.

5. **Empathy:** An empathetic protagonist can evoke compassion and understanding from the audience. Their empathy allows them to connect with other characters, build relationships, and make morally sound decisions, enhancing the emotional impact of their journey.

Framework for a protagonist's journey of completing tasks and unveiling destiny.

1. **Call to Adventure:** The protagonist receives a call to embark on their journey, setting the stage for their tasks and destiny. This call could come from a mentor, a prophecy, or an inciting incident that propels them forward.

2. **Task Completion:** The protagonist encounters a series of tasks or challenges that they must overcome. These tasks push them beyond their comfort zone, test their abilities, and contribute to their personal growth and understanding of their destiny.

3. **Allies and Antagonists:** The protagonist forms alliances with supporting characters who aid them in completing tasks

and understanding their destiny. They also encounter antagonists who provide obstacles, conflicts, and growth opportunities.

4. **Revelation and Transformation:** As the protagonist completes tasks and unravels their destiny, they experience moments of revelation and self-discovery. These moments lead to transformation, where they gain new insights, change their perspectives, and evolve as individuals.

5. **Resolution:** The protagonist's journey reaches a resolution where they fulfill their tasks, embrace their destiny, or come to a new understanding of themselves. This resolution provides closure to the narrative arc and leaves the audience with a sense of satisfaction.

Advantages for a protagonist's journey of completing tasks and unveiling destiny.

1. **Emotional Engagement:** A protagonist's journey can evoke strong emotions in the audience, such as excitement, suspense, and satisfaction. This emotional engagement enhances the overall enjoyment and impact of the story.

2. **Character Development:** The journey allows for significant character development, as the protagonist faces challenges, grows, and evolves. This depth of character adds complexity and relatability, making the story more compelling.

3. **Narrative Tension:** The completion of tasks and the unveiling of destiny create narrative tension and suspense.

The audience eagerly follows the protagonist's progress, anticipating the outcome and staying engaged in the story.

4. **Themes and Messages:** Through the journey, themes and messages can be explored, such as the power of determination, the importance of self-discovery, or the consequences of choices. These themes add depth and resonance to the narrative.

5. **Sense of Accomplishment:** As the protagonist completes tasks and unveils their destiny, there is a sense of accomplishment for both the character and the audience. This provides a satisfying narrative arc and a feeling of closure.

Disadvantages for a protagonist's journey of completing tasks and unveiling destiny.

1. **Predictability:** A protagonist's journey of completing tasks and unveiling destiny can sometimes become predictable, especially if it follows a formulaic structure. This may reduce the element of surprise and diminish the impact on the audience.

2. **Lack of Originality:** If the journey and tasks are overly familiar or clichéd, it can detract from the uniqueness and freshness of the story. The audience may feel that they have seen similar narratives before, leading to a diminished impact.

3. **Pacing Challenges:** Balancing the completion of tasks and the unveiling of destiny can present pacing challenges. If the

story moves too slowly or too quickly, it may affect the audience's engagement and immersion in the narrative.

4. **Unrealistic Progression:** The journey may involve unrealistic advancements or achievements for the protagonist. If tasks are completed too easily or without sufficient build-up, it can undermine the believability and immersion of the story.

5. **Lack of Agency:** In some cases, the protagonist's journey may lack agency if they are simply following a predetermined path or fulfilling tasks without active decision-making. This can diminish the sense of empowerment and personal investment for both the character and the audience.

Chapter 13: The protagonist's daily agenda for missionary.

Here is a sample daily agenda for a protagonist engaged in a missionary role.

Morning.

1. Wake up and engage in personal devotional time, including prayer and meditation.
2. Prepare for the day by getting dressed appropriately for the missionary work.
3. Have a healthy breakfast to fuel the body for the day ahead.
4. Review the schedule and tasks for the day.

Mid-Morning.

1. Engage in community outreach activities, such as visiting local families, conducting Bible studies, or providing assistance to those in need.
2. Share the message of faith and provide spiritual guidance to individuals or groups encountered during outreach activities.

3. Connect with local religious leaders or community members to establish relationships and collaborations.

Lunchtime.

1. Take a break for lunch and have a wholesome meal.
2. Use this time to reflect on the morning's activities and plan for the rest of the day.

Afternoon.

1. Continue with community outreach activities, focusing on specific needs or projects, such as organizing educational programs, health initiatives, or social services.
2. Conduct meetings or training sessions with local volunteers or fellow missionaries to discuss strategies, share experiences, and provide support.
3. Engage in language learning or cultural immersion activities to better connect with the local community.

Evening.

1. Wrap up the day's activities and review any unfinished tasks or follow-ups required.
2. Engage in personal reflection and journaling, documenting experiences, insights, and challenges encountered during the day.
3. Attend or participate in local religious services or gatherings to further connect with the community.

4. Spend time bonding with fellow missionaries, discussing the day's experiences, and providing mutual support.

Night.

1. Have a nutritious dinner to replenish energy.
2. Engage in personal time for relaxation, self-care, or hobbies.
3. Engage in further study or preparation for upcoming missionary work.
4. End the day with personal reflection, gratitude, and prayer.

Tips of the protagonist's daily agenda for missionary.

1. **Embrace Cultural Sensitivity:** Respect and appreciate the local culture, traditions, and customs of the community you are serving.
2. **Build Relationships:** Focus on building genuine relationships with the local community, listening to their needs, and working collaboratively to address them.
3. **Flexibility and Adaptability:** Be open to unexpected changes or challenges, and be willing to adjust plans accordingly.
4. **Continuous Learning:** Seek opportunities to learn about the local language, customs, and history, as it helps in effective communication and building trust.
5. **Self-Care and Rest:** Take care of your physical, emotional, and spiritual well-being to sustain yourself throughout the missionary journey.

Benefits of Missionary Work.

1. **Spiritual Growth:** Engaging in missionary work allows for personal spiritual growth, deepening one's faith and understanding of different cultures and beliefs.

2. **Impact on Others:** Missionary work provides the opportunity to make a positive impact on the lives of individuals and communities, offering support, hope, and guidance.

3. **Cross-Cultural Understanding:** Engaging with diverse communities fosters cross-cultural understanding, promoting tolerance, empathy, and global awareness.

4. **Personal Development:** Missionary work enhances skills such as communication, adaptability, leadership, and problem-solving, contributing to personal growth and resilience.

5. **Fulfillment and Purpose:** Engaging in missionary work often brings a sense of fulfillment, purpose, and a deeper connection to one's faith and calling.

Functions of the protagonist's daily agenda for missionary.

1. **Outreach and Evangelism:** Spreading the message of faith and offering spiritual guidance to individuals and communities.

2. **Community Development:** Engaging in initiatives that promote education, healthcare, social services, and other forms of community development.

3. **Cultural Exchange:** Facilitating cultural exchange and understanding between different communities, fostering mutual respect and appreciation.

4. **Humanitarian Aid:** Assisting those in need, including access to food, clean water, medical care, and other essential resources.

5. **Discipleship and Mentorship:** Mentoring and nurturing individuals in their faith journey, offering guidance and support for personal growth and spiritual development.

Techniques of the protagonist's daily agenda for missionary.

1. **Effective Communication:** Utilize active listening, empathy, and clear communication to connect with individuals and communities.

2. **Cultural Sensitivity:** Respect and appreciate the local culture, traditions, and customs, adapting communication and practices accordingly.

3. **Relationship Building:** Foster genuine relationships with community members, demonstrating care, trust, and respect.

4. **Collaboration:** Work collaboratively with local volunteers, community leaders, and organizations to maximize impact and sustainability.

5. **Empowerment:** Encourage and empower individuals within the community to take ownership of their development and growth.

Factors of the protagonist's daily agenda for missionary.

1. **Faith and Belief:** The missionary's faith and belief in their mission and purpose play a significant role in driving their work.

2. **Cultural Context:** Understanding and adapting to the cultural context in which the missionary operates is crucial for effective engagement.

3. **Socioeconomic Factors:** Socioeconomic conditions, including poverty, access to education, healthcare, and basic needs, can shape the missionary's work and impact.

4. **Political Climate:** The political climate of the region or country can impact the opportunities and challenges faced by the missionary.

5. **Support System:** The presence of a supportive network, including fellow missionaries, local volunteers, and organizations, can greatly influence the success of the missionary's work.

Causes of the protagonist's daily agenda for missionary.

1. **Personal Calling:** Many missionaries are driven by a personal calling or conviction to serve and make a positive impact in the world.

2. **Compassion and Empathy:** A deep sense of compassion and empathy for those in need motivates missionaries to alleviate suffering and offer support.

3. **Religious or Spiritual Beliefs:** Religious or spiritual beliefs can be a driving force behind a missionary's desire to spread their faith and provide spiritual guidance.
4. **Desire for Social Justice:** The desire to address social injustices, and inequality, and promote human rights can inspire missionaries to engage in their work.
5. **Humanitarian Concerns:** Concern for the well-being and holistic development of individuals and communities often drives missionaries to provide humanitarian aid and support.

Importance of Missionary Work.

1. **Spreading Faith:** Missionary work plays a crucial role in spreading and sharing one's faith with others.
2. **Humanitarian Aid:** Missionaries often provide essential aid, such as healthcare, education, and social services, to improve the lives of individuals and communities.
3. **Cultural Exchange:** Engaging with different cultures fosters mutual understanding, respect, and appreciation for diversity.
4. **Personal Transformation:** Missionary work allows individuals to grow spiritually, develop empathy, and gain a broader perspective on the world.
5. **Community Development:** Missionaries contribute to the development of communities by addressing social, economic, and spiritual needs.

Qualities of the protagonist's daily agenda for missionary.

1. **Strong Faith:** A deep and unwavering faith in their beliefs, which serves as the foundation for their missionary work.

2. **Empathy and Compassion:** The ability to understand and connect with the struggles and needs of others, demonstrating genuine care and compassion.

3. **Cultural Sensitivity:** Respect and appreciation for different cultures, customs, and traditions, adapting their approach accordingly.

4. **Adaptability and Flexibility:** Being open to change, embracing challenges, and adjusting plans to effectively respond to varying situations.

5. **Strong Work Ethic:** A committed and dedicated work ethic to persistently serve others and make a positive impact.

Framework of the protagonist's daily agenda for missionary.

1. **Outreach and Evangelism:** Sharing the message of faith and providing spiritual guidance to individuals and communities.

2. **Community Engagement:** Actively engaging with the local community, building relationships, and addressing their unique needs.

3. **Education and Empowerment:** Providing resources, knowledge, and skills to empower individuals and communities for sustainable development.

4. **Holistic Approach:** Addressing physical, emotional, social, and spiritual needs to foster holistic well-being.

5. **Collaboration and Partnerships:** Working with local organizations, churches, and volunteers to maximize impact and create lasting change.

Advantages of the protagonist's daily agenda for missionary.

1. **Spiritual fulfillment:** Engaging in missionary work can provide the protagonist with a deep sense of purpose and spiritual fulfillment.

2. **Cultural immersion:** Missionary work often involves traveling to different countries and communities, allowing the protagonist to experience and learn about diverse cultures firsthand.

3. **Making a difference:** Missionaries have the opportunity to positively impact the lives of individuals and communities by offering support, and assistance, and spreading their message of faith.

4. **Personal growth:** Through missionary work, the protagonist can develop valuable skills such as empathy, communication, adaptability, and intercultural understanding.

5. **Building relationships:** Missionaries often build strong relationships with the locals they serve, creating lasting bonds and a sense of community.

Disadvantages of the protagonist's daily agenda for missionary.

1. **Language barrier:** Depending on the location of the mission, the protagonist may face difficulties in

communicating effectively with the community due to
language barriers.

2. **Cultural challenges:** Adapting to a new culture can be
   overwhelming and challenging, leading to potential
   misunderstandings and cultural clashes.

3. **Lack of resources:** Some missionary destinations may lack
   basic amenities and resources, making it difficult for the
   protagonist to carry out their work effectively.

4. **Homesickness:** Being away from friends, family, and the
   comforts of home can lead to feelings of homesickness and
   loneliness for the protagonist.

5. **Safety risks:** In certain locations, missionaries may face
   potential risks to their safety and security, such as political
   instability, natural disasters, or hostility towards their
   religious beliefs.

Chapter 14: The Crucial Role of Protagonists.

Shaping Narratives and Inspiring Change.

Protagonists play a pivotal role in shaping and driving narratives across various forms of literature, film, and storytelling. They serve as the central characters who guide the audience through their journeys, experiences, and transformations. The most crucial job of protagonists lies in their ability to captivate audiences, convey themes, and inspire change within the story's context. In this chapter we delve into the significance of protagonists, exploring their role in creating engaging narratives, embodying archetypal qualities, and catalyzing personal and societal transformations.

1. Captivating Audiences.

Protagonists possess the power to captivate audiences through their relatability and compelling stories. By presenting characters with whom viewers or readers can connect, protagonists create an emotional bond, drawing the audience into the narrative. Their struggles, triumphs, and growth keep the audience invested, fostering an immersive experience that deepens their connection with the story.

2. Conveying Themes.

Protagonists often serve as conduits for conveying overarching themes and messages within a narrative. Through their actions, decisions, and interactions, they embody the values, conflicts, and dilemmas explored in the story. By personifying these themes, protagonists enable audiences to engage with abstract concepts on a more personal and relatable level, facilitating reflection and deeper understanding.

3. Embodying Archetypal Qualities.

Protagonists frequently embody archetypal qualities, representing universal traits and characteristics that resonate with audiences across different cultures and periods. From the hero's journey to the underdog overcoming obstacles, archetypal protagonists provide a framework for storytelling that taps into shared human experiences. They inspire and empower audiences by reflecting the potential for growth, resilience, and transformation within each individual.

4. Catalyzing Personal Transformations.

One of the most significant roles of protagonists lies in their ability to catalyze personal transformations, both within the story and in the audience. As protagonists face challenges, they undergo profound character development, often overcoming internal and external obstacles. By witnessing their journeys, audiences are encouraged to reflect on their own lives and growth potential. Protagonists serve as catalysts for self-reflection, inspiring individuals to confront their fears, embrace change, and embark on their transformative journeys.

5. Inspiring Societal Change.

Beyond personal transformations, protagonists can also inspire societal change. Through their struggles against injustice, oppression, or societal norms, protagonists challenge the status quo and ignite conversations about social issues. By embodying the values of courage, compassion, and resilience, they encourage audiences to question prevailing systems and advocate for positive change. Protagonists become symbols of hope, inspiring individuals to stand up for their beliefs and work towards a better future.

Tips for Creating Effective Protagonists.

1. **Establish Clear Goals and Motivations:** Give your protagonist a compelling reason to embark on their journey. Clearly define their goals and motivations, ensuring they align with the central conflict of the narrative. This will engage the audience and drive the story forward.

2. **Develop Complex and Multi-Dimensional Characters:** Create protagonists with depth and complexity. Give them strengths, flaws, and internal conflicts that make them relatable and believable. This complexity adds nuance to their journey and makes their transformation more impactful.

3. **Provide Opportunities for Growth and Development:**
   Design challenges and obstacles that force your protagonist
   to confront their weaknesses and evolve. Allow them to learn
   from their experiences and make meaningful changes,
   fostering personal growth and transformation.

4. **Foster Emotional Connection:** Craft protagonists that evoke
   empathy and emotional investment from the audience.
   Develop their backstory, relationships, and vulnerabilities to
   evoke a range of emotions, creating a strong bond between
   the audience and the character.

5. **Show Agency and Active Participation:** Ensure your
   protagonist is an active participant in the story, driving the
   plot forward through their choices and actions. Avoid making
   them passive observers or victims of circumstance.
   Protagonists who take charge and make decisions inspire and
   engage the audience.

Benefits of Well-Developed Protagonists.

1. **Audience Engagement:** Strong protagonists captivate
   audiences, keeping them invested in the narrative. When
   audiences connect with well-developed characters, they
   become emotionally involved and more likely to follow the
   story to its resolution.

2. **Memorable and Impactful Stories:** Protagonists who
   undergo significant transformations or achieve remarkable
   goals leave a lasting impression on audiences. Their journeys

resonate deeply, making the story more memorable and impactful.

3. **Exploration of Themes and Values:** Through the protagonist's experiences, stories can explore important themes and values. Protagonists act as conduits, allowing audiences to reflect on moral, philosophical, or societal questions, fostering deeper understanding and discussion.

4. **Inspiration and Empowerment:** Protagonists who overcome challenges and obstacles inspire audiences, instilling a sense of hope and empowerment. Witnessing characters triumph over adversity encourages individuals to face their challenges with resilience and determination.

5. **Catalyst for Change:** Well-developed protagonists can act as catalysts for personal and societal change. By embodying virtues, challenging norms, or fighting against injustice, they inspire audiences to question the status quo and take action, fostering positive transformation.

Functions of Protagonists in Narratives.

1. **Driving the Plot:** Protagonists propel the story forward through their actions, decisions, and goals. They provide the central focus around which the narrative revolves.

2. **Conflict Creation:** Protagonists often find themselves in conflict with antagonistic forces or face internal conflicts. These conflicts create tension and drive the narrative's momentum.

3. **Character Development:** The protagonists undergo personal growth and transformation throughout the story. Their experiences, challenges, and choices shape their development, adding depth and complexity to their character.

4. **Theme Representation:** Protagonists embody the themes and values explored in the narrative, serving as vehicles for their exploration and expression. Their actions and choices reflect and convey the story's underlying messages.

5. **Audience Identification:** Protagonists provide a relatable character through whom audiences can experience the narrative. Audiences connect with protagonists, identifying with their struggles, aspirations, and emotions, enhancing their engagement with the story.

Techniques for Crafting Protagonists.

1. **Character Arc:** Develop a clear character arc for your protagonist, ensuring they undergo significant growth and transformation throughout the story. Create a compelling journey that challenges their beliefs, values, and abilities, leading to personal development.

2. **Flawed but Relatable:** Make your protagonist relatable by giving them flaws and vulnerabilities. Flawed characters are more compelling and allow audiences to connect on a deeper level, as they see reflections of their imperfections.

3. **Inner Conflict:** Introduce inner conflicts within your protagonist, such as conflicting desires, moral dilemmas, or unresolved traumas. This adds depth and complexity to their

character, driving their internal struggle and providing growth opportunities.

4. **Strong Motivation:** Ensure your protagonist has a clear and strong motivation that drives their actions and decisions. This motivation should align with the story's central conflict and resonate with the audience, evoking empathy and investment.

5. **Unique Voice and Perspective:** Give your protagonist a unique voice and perspective that distinguishes them from other characters. This helps them stand out and adds authenticity to their portrayal, making them memorable to the audience.

Factors Influencing Protagonist Effectiveness.

1. **Conflict:** The nature and intensity of the conflicts faced by the protagonist significantly impact their effectiveness. Engaging conflicts challenges the protagonist's goals, values, or beliefs, creating opportunities for growth and compelling storytelling.

2. **Supporting Characters:** The quality and dynamics of the relationships between the protagonist and supporting characters contribute to their effectiveness. Well-developed supporting characters provide depth, conflict, and emotional support to the protagonist, enhancing the overall narrative.

3. **Setting:** The setting in which the protagonist operates can influence their effectiveness. A richly detailed and immersive setting can enhance the protagonist's journey, creating opportunities for exploration, conflict, and personal growth.

4. **Stakes:** The stakes associated with the protagonist's actions and choices influence their effectiveness. Higher stakes increase tension and create a sense of urgency, making the protagonist's journey more engaging and impactful.

5. **Theme Relevance:** The extent to which the protagonist embodies and reflects the themes explored in the narrative affects their effectiveness. When the protagonist's journey aligns with the central themes and values of the story, their actions and transformation resonate more deeply with the audience.

Causes of Protagonist Impact.

1. **Emotional Connection:** Protagonists who evoke strong emotions in the audience, such as empathy, admiration, or inspiration, have a greater impact. Emotional resonance fosters a deeper connection between the audience and the protagonist, making their journey more impactful.

2. **Identification and Relatability:** Protagonists who exhibit qualities, experiences, or struggles similar to those of the audience are more likely to have a lasting impact. When audiences see themselves in the protagonist, they become personally invested in their journey and outcomes.

3. **Narrative Arc:** A well-structured narrative arc that effectively highlights the protagonist's growth, challenges, and triumphs contributes to their impact. A satisfying narrative structure allows audiences to witness the

protagonist's transformation and provides closure, leaving a
lasting impression.

4. **Symbolism and Archetypes:** Protagonists who embody
   symbolic or archetypal qualities can have a profound impact.
   These characters represent universal themes and tap into
   collective unconsciousness, resonating with audiences across
   cultures and generations.

5. **Social and Cultural Relevance:** Protagonists who address
   or challenge social, cultural, or political issues have the
   potential to make a significant impact. By reflecting
   contemporary or timeless concerns, they inspire discussions,
   provoke thought, and motivate change.

**Importance of Protagonists in Shaping Narratives and Inspiring
Change.**

1. **Central Focus:** Protagonists serve as the central focus of a
   narrative, anchoring the story and providing a point of
   identification for audiences. They guide the audience through
   their experiences, emotions, and growth, keeping them
   engaged and invested in the narrative.

2. **Emotional Connection:** Protagonists evoke emotions and
   create a strong emotional bond with the audience. By
   experiencing the protagonist's journey vicariously, audiences
   become emotionally invested, fostering a deeper connection
   and enhancing the impact of the narrative.

3. **Driving the Plot:** Protagonists drive the plot forward through
   their goals, actions, and decisions. Their pursuit of objectives

and the conflicts they encounter create tension and momentum, propelling the narrative toward its resolution.

4. **Catalyst for Change:** Protagonists have the power to inspire change, both within the story and in the audience. Through their struggles, growth, and triumphs, they can motivate viewers or readers to reevaluate their own lives, beliefs, or societal norms, sparking personal and societal transformations.

5. **Reflection of Human Experience:** Protagonists reflect the complexities of the human experience, exploring universal themes, struggles, and triumphs. They provide a lens through which audiences can reflect on their own lives, values, and aspirations, fostering empathy and understanding.

Qualities of Memorable Protagonists.

1. **Relatability:** Memorable protagonists are relatable, possessing qualities, flaws, and aspirations that resonate with the audience. Their relatability allows audiences to connect on a personal level, forming a lasting impression.

2. **Complexity:** Protagonists with depth and complexity are more memorable. They possess multidimensional characteristics, inner conflicts, and nuanced motivations, making them intriguing and realistic.

3. **Growth and Transformation:** Memorable protagonists undergo significant growth and transformation throughout the narrative. Their development, fueled by challenges and experiences, adds depth and impact to their character arc.

4. **Agency and Determination:** Protagonists who exhibit agency and determination are memorable. Their proactive nature and resilience in the face of adversity inspire audiences, leaving a lasting impression.

5. **Unique Voice and Perspective:** Memorable protagonists have a distinct voice and perspective that sets them apart. Their unique qualities, quirks, or worldviews make them stand out, leaving a mark on the audience's memory.

Frameworks for Protagonist Development.

1. **The Hero's Journey:** The hero's journey framework, popularized by Joseph Campbell, outlines the stages of a protagonist's transformational journey. It provides a structured framework for character development, incorporating key elements such as the call to adventure, mentors, trials, and ultimate transformation.

2. **Archetypal Character Models:** Utilizing archetypal character models, such as the Hero, the Rebel, or the Sage, provides a framework for constructing memorable protagonists. These archetypes embody universal qualities and resonate with audiences across cultures and time.

3. **Three-Dimensional Characterization:** Developing three-dimensional characters involves providing protagonists with a well-rounded personality, including strengths, weaknesses, desires, and fears. This framework helps create realistic and relatable characters.

4. **Motivation-Conflict-Resolution:** The motivation-conflict-resolution framework focuses on ensuring that the protagonist's motivations align with the central conflict of the narrative. By structuring the story around this framework, the protagonist's journey becomes more cohesive and impactful.

5. **Theme-Driven Characterization:** In theme-driven characterization, the protagonist's qualities, choices, and actions are intentionally aligned with the themes explored in the narrative. This framework ensures that the protagonist serves as a vehicle for conveying and exploring the story's central themes.

Advantages of Protagonists in Shaping Narratives and Inspiring Change.

1. **Engaging Audience:** Protagonists captivate audiences and keep them invested in the story. Their compelling journeys, emotions, and growth draw viewers or readers into the narrative, enhancing engagement and enjoyment.

2. **Emotional Connection:** Protagonists evoke emotions and create a strong emotional bond with the audience. Through their struggles and triumphs, they elicit empathy, compassion, and inspiration, fostering a deeper connection and enhancing the impact of the narrative.

3. **Driving the Plot:** Protagonists serve as the driving force of the narrative, propelling the plot forward through their goals, actions, and decisions. Their pursuit of objectives and the

conflicts they encounter create tension, suspense, and momentum, keeping the audience engaged and eager to know the outcome.

4. **Inspiring Change:** Protagonists have the power to inspire change, both within the story and in the audience. By overcoming obstacles, challenging norms, or embodying virtues, they motivate viewers or readers to question the status quo, reevaluate their own lives, and strive for personal growth or positive societal transformations.

5. **Memorable and Impactful Stories:** Well-crafted protagonists leave a lasting impression on audiences. Their compelling journeys, growth, and impact resonate deeply, making the story more memorable, thought-provoking, and impactful.

Disadvantages of Protagonists in Shaping Narratives and Inspiring Change.

1. **Overused Tropes:** Protagonists can become predictable or stereotypical if they adhere too closely to common character tropes or archetypes. This can lead to a lack of originality or depth, making the story and its messages less impactful.

2. **Lack of Diversity:** If protagonists consistently represent a narrow range of identities or perspectives, it can limit the ability of the narrative to resonate with a diverse audience. This may exclude or marginalize certain groups, hindering the potential for broad-reaching impact.

3. **Unrealistic Portrayals:** Protagonists who are portrayed as overly idealized or flawless may create a disconnection between the audience and the character. If the protagonist's journey or transformation feels unrealistic or unattainable, it can diminish their ability to inspire change.

4. **One-Dimensional Characters:** Protagonists that lack complexity or depth can be less engaging and relatable. If their motivations, behaviors, or growth are underdeveloped, it may weaken the impact of their actions and hinder the audience's emotional connection.

5. **Misaligned Messages:** If the actions or beliefs of the protagonist contradict or undermine the intended messages or themes of the narrative, it can lead to confusion or a lack of resonance with the audience. This may dilute the potential for inspiring meaningful change.

Chapter 15: Unveiling the Protagonist's Narrative.

A Journey of Growth and Transformation.

The narrative is a powerful tool that allows us to delve into the depths of a story, unraveling the complexities and intricacies of the characters involved. Among these characters, the protagonist stands at the forefront, guiding us through the story's twists and turns. The protagonist's narrative is a captivating exploration of their experiences, emotions, and growth. This chapter aims to examine the significance of the protagonist's narrative in storytelling, highlighting how it shapes the overall plot, engages readers, and portrays the protagonist's journey of self-discovery, challenges, and transformation. Through a comprehensive analysis of various literary works and their protagonists, we will uncover the profound impact of the protagonist's narrative on the overall storytelling experience.

1. Defining the Protagonist's Narrative.

- The protagonist's role in storytelling.
- Understanding the narrative perspective.

- The protagonist's influence on the plot development.

2. Engaging the Reader.

- Establishing a strong connection with the protagonist.
- Emotional investment in the protagonist's journey.
- Reader identification and empathy.

3. Unveiling the Protagonist's Journey.

- Introducing the protagonist's aspirations, desires, and flaws.
- Presenting the protagonist's challenges and conflicts.
- Tracing the protagonist's growth and development.
- Examining key turning points and their impact on the narrative.

4. The Power of Perspective.

- **First-person narrative:** Immersion and introspection.
- **Third-person limited:** Balancing insight and distance.
- **Multiple perspectives:** Expanding the narrative canvas.

5. Themes Explored through the Protagonist's Narrative.

- Identity and self-discovery.
- Resilience and overcoming adversity.
- Moral dilemmas and ethical choices.
- Love, loss, and relationships.

6. Symbolism and Imagery in the Protagonist's Narrative.

- Symbolic motifs and their significance.
- Metaphors and allegories.
- Use of vivid imagery to enhance the narrative.

7. Breaking Stereotypes through the Protagonist's Narrative.

- Challenging gender and cultural norms.
- Defying societal expectations.
- Empowering marginalized voices.

8. Protagonist's Narrative in Different Genres.

- Protagonist in fantasy and science fiction.
- Protagonist in mystery and crime novels.
- Protagonist in historical fiction and biographies.

Tips for Unveiling the Protagonist's Narrative.

1. **Establish a Strong Character Foundation:** Lay a solid foundation for your protagonist by developing their personality, backstory, and motivations. This will provide a clear understanding of who they are and what drives them, setting the stage for their narrative journey.

2. **Create Conflict and Challenges:** Introduce obstacles and conflicts that the protagonist must face throughout the story. These challenges can be internal or external, pushing the

protagonist to their limits and forcing them to grow and change.

3. **Show Emotional Depth:** Explore the protagonist's emotions and inner thoughts to create a deep connection between the reader and the character. By revealing their vulnerabilities, fears, and desires, you allow readers to empathize with the protagonist and become invested in their narrative.

4. **Highlight Transformative Moments:** Identify key turning points in the protagonist's journey where they undergo significant growth or transformation. These moments can be pivotal events, realizations, or decisions that shape the narrative and contribute to the protagonist's development.

5. **Provide Resolution and Closure:** Ensure that the protagonist's narrative arc reaches a satisfying conclusion. Tie up loose ends, address unanswered questions, and allow the protagonist to achieve their goals or find closure. This provides a sense of fulfillment for readers and completes the protagonist's transformative journey.

Benefits of Unveiling the Protagonist's Narrative.

1. **Emotional Engagement:** When readers connect with the protagonist on an emotional level, they become more invested in the story. Understanding the protagonist's narrative allows readers to experience a range of emotions and form a deeper connection with the characters.

2. **Empathy and Understanding:** Unveiling the protagonist's narrative provides insights into their thoughts, feelings, and

experiences. This fosters empathy and understanding, allowing readers to gain a broader perspective on different life journeys and diverse perspectives.

3. **Personal Growth and Inspiration:** Through the protagonist's transformative journey, readers can find inspiration and learn valuable life lessons. Witnessing the protagonist's growth and transformation can encourage readers to reflect on their own lives and embark on their journeys of self-discovery and development.

4. **Narrative Coherence:** The protagonist's narrative serves as a thread that binds the story together. By unraveling their journey, the narrative gains coherence and purpose, creating a more engaging and satisfying reading experience.

5. **Exploration of Complex Themes:** The protagonist's narrative often serves as a vehicle to explore complex themes such as identity, morality, and societal issues. By delving into the protagonist's experiences and challenges, readers can contemplate these themes on a deeper level, expanding their understanding of the human condition.

Functions of the Protagonist's Narrative.

1. **Plot Advancement:** The protagonist's narrative propels the plot forward, as their actions and decisions have significant consequences. The protagonist's journey often intertwines with the central conflict, shaping the story's trajectory and outcome.

2. **Character Development:** Through the protagonist's narrative, readers witness their growth, transformation, and evolution. This allows for a multi-dimensional portrayal of the characters, revealing their strengths, weaknesses, and complexities.

3. **Reader Identification:** The protagonist's narrative provides readers with a relatable point of reference. Readers can identify with the protagonist's struggles, aspirations, and emotions, creating a deeper sense of engagement and connection with the story.

4. **Theme Exploration:** The protagonist's narrative offers a platform to explore and examine various themes and ideas. Their experiences and choices can shed light on broader concepts, enabling readers to contemplate societal issues, moral dilemmas, and personal values.

5. **Catharsis and Emotional Impact:** The protagonist's narrative has the power to evoke strong emotions in readers. By experiencing the protagonist's journey, readers can undergo a cathartic release and emotional catharsis, leading to a more profound and memorable reading experience.

Techniques for Unveiling the Protagonist's Narrative.

1. **Character Interiority:** Employ techniques such as internal monologues, introspection, and stream of consciousness to reveal the protagonist's thoughts, emotions, and inner conflicts. This technique offers readers a direct window into

the protagonist's mind, fostering a deeper understanding of their journey.

2. **Dialogue:** Utilize dialogue to showcase the protagonist's interactions with other characters. Through conversations, readers can gain insights into the protagonist's relationships, beliefs, and motivations, adding depth to their narrative.

3. **Flashbacks and Memories:** Incorporate flashbacks or memories to provide glimpses into the protagonist's past. This technique allows readers to uncover formative experiences, traumas, or significant events that have shaped the protagonist's current state, enhancing their narrative development.

4. **Symbolism and Metaphor:** Employ symbolic elements and metaphors to convey the protagonist's inner struggles, desires, or transformation. Symbolism adds layers of meaning to the narrative, inviting readers to interpret the protagonist's journey on a metaphorical level.

5. **Foreshadowing:** Use foreshadowing to hint at future events or character developments. By subtly alluding to upcoming challenges or transformations, readers are prepared for the protagonist's narrative arc, creating anticipation and engagement.

Factors Influencing the Protagonist's Narrative.

1. **External Environment:** The setting, society, and cultural context in which the protagonist exists can greatly influence their narrative. External factors such as social norms,

political events, or geographical landscapes can shape the protagonist's challenges, choices, and opportunities for growth.

2. **Relationships and Interactions:** The protagonist's relationships with other characters play a crucial role in their narrative. Positive or toxic relationships, friendships, or romantic connections can impact the protagonist's emotional journey and shape their transformation.

3. **Personal Agency:** The protagonist's agency and choices significantly impact their narrative. The decisions they make, the risks they take, and the actions they pursue contribute to their growth and transformation throughout the story.

4. **Internal Conflicts:** The protagonist's internal conflicts, such as moral dilemmas, unresolved traumas, or conflicting desires, affect their narrative trajectory. These internal struggles create tension and drive the protagonist's journey of self-discovery and transformation.

5. **Goals and Motivations:** The protagonist's goals and motivations provide a driving force for their narrative. Whether it's seeking justice, love, power, or personal fulfillment, the protagonist's desires shape their actions and influence the direction of their journey.

Causes of the Protagonist's Transformation.

1. **Crisis or Traumatic Events:** A significant crisis or trauma can act as a catalyst for the protagonist's transformation. Confronting adversity or experiencing a life-altering event

forces the protagonist to reassess their beliefs, values, and priorities.

2. **Mentorship or Guidance:** The presence of a mentor or guide can profoundly impact the protagonist's narrative. The mentor's wisdom, teachings, and support can inspire personal growth, leading to a transformative journey for the protagonist.

3. **Self-Reflection and Introspection:** Moments of self-reflection and introspection prompt the protagonist to question their beliefs, motivations, and actions. This self-examination fosters personal growth and facilitates transformative change.

4. **Overcoming Challenges:** Navigating and overcoming challenges and obstacles tests the protagonist's resilience and determination. The process of overcoming adversity often leads to the protagonist's growth, as they learn valuable lessons and develop new strengths.

5. **Epiphany or Revelation:** The protagonist may experience a moment of epiphany or revelation that shatters their previous worldview or understanding. This sudden realization or insight can spark a transformative shift in their perspective, values, or goals.

Importance of Unveiling the Protagonist's Narrative.

1. **Emotional Connection:** Unveiling the protagonist's narrative allows readers to form an emotional bond with the character. This connection enhances reader engagement and

investment in the story, making it more compelling and memorable.

2. **Character Development:** The protagonist's narrative serves as a platform for their development and transformation. By exploring their journey, readers witness the protagonist's growth, flaws, and strengths, creating well-rounded and relatable characters.

3. **Theme Exploration:** The protagonist's narrative provides an avenue for exploring complex themes and ideas. Through their experiences and challenges, readers can contemplate and reflect upon broader concepts such as identity, morality, and societal norms.

4. **Empathy and Understanding:** Unveiling the protagonist's narrative fosters empathy and understanding among readers. By delving into the character's thoughts, emotions, and struggles, readers gain a deeper understanding of different perspectives and life experiences.

5. **Inspirational and Reflective Value:** The protagonist's transformative journey can inspire readers to reflect on their own lives and personal growth. By witnessing the protagonist's challenges and triumphs, readers may find motivation and insight to embark on their transformative journeys.

Qualities of a Compelling Protagonist's Narrative.

1. **Complexity:** A compelling protagonist's narrative showcases a multi-dimensional character with depth and

complexity. They possess a combination of strengths, weaknesses, flaws, and virtues that make them relatable and interesting.

2. **Growth and Transformation:** The protagonist's narrative should demonstrate their growth and transformation throughout the story. They evolve, learn from their experiences, and undergo personal development, capturing readers' attention and investment.

3. **Authenticity:** A compelling protagonist's narrative is authentic to the character's personality. Their thoughts, actions, and choices align with their established traits, allowing readers to connect with them on a genuine level.

4. **Conflict and Challenges:** The protagonist's narrative should be filled with conflicts and challenges that they must face and overcome. These obstacles serve as catalysts for growth and provide opportunities for the protagonist to showcase their resilience and determination.

5. **Relatability:** A compelling protagonist's narrative resonates with readers by reflecting universal human experiences and emotions. Their struggles, desires, and aspirations strike a chord with readers, making them relatable and compelling.

Framework for Unveiling the Protagonist's Narrative.

1. **Establishing the Protagonist's Background:** Introduce the protagonist's background, including their past experiences, relationships, and motivations. This framework helps readers

understand the character's starting point and establishes a foundation for their narrative journey.

2. **Introducing Conflict and Challenges:** Present conflicts and challenges that the protagonist must confront. These obstacles create tension and drive the narrative forward, setting the stage for the protagonist's growth and transformation.

3. **Development of Internal and External Factors:** Develop the internal and external factors that shape the protagonist's narrative. This framework includes their internal struggles, relationships with other characters, and the impact of the external environment on their journey.

4. **Narrative Arc:** Structure the protagonist's narrative using a clear arc, including exposition, rising action, climax, falling action, and resolution. This framework guides the progression of the protagonist's journey and ensures a satisfying narrative structure.

5. **Reflection and Resolution:** Allow the protagonist moments of reflection and introspection throughout their narrative. These moments provide opportunities for the protagonist to process their experiences, make choices, and ultimately reach a resolution or transformational conclusion.

Advantages of Unveiling the Protagonist's Narrative.

1. **Emotional Engagement:** Unveiling the protagonist's narrative allows readers to form a deep emotional connection with the character. This emotional engagement enhances

reader investment in the story and creates a more immersive and impactful reading experience.

2. **Character Development:** By revealing the protagonist's narrative, readers witness their growth and transformation throughout the story. This provides a rich and dynamic character arc, making the protagonist more relatable and compelling.

3. **Theme Exploration:** The protagonist's narrative offers an opportunity to explore complex themes and ideas. Through their journey, readers can contemplate and reflect upon broader concepts such as identity, morality, and personal growth.

4. **Empathy and Understanding:** Unveiling the protagonist's narrative fosters empathy and understanding among readers. By delving into the character's thoughts, emotions, and struggles, readers gain a deeper understanding of different perspectives and the human condition.

5. **Inspirational Value:** The protagonist's transformative journey can inspire readers to reflect on their own lives and personal growth. Witnessing the protagonist's challenges and triumphs can provide motivation and insight for readers to embark on their transformative journeys.

Disadvantages of Unveiling the Protagonist's Narrative.

1. **Predictability:** When the protagonist's narrative is too predictable, it can diminish the impact and surprise factor of their growth and transformation. Readers may anticipate the

character's arc, leading to a less engaging reading experience.

2. **Lack of Depth:** If the protagonist's narrative is not adequately explored, their growth and transformation may feel superficial or underdeveloped. This can hinder reader engagement and make the character's journey less impactful.

3. **Imbalance with Supporting Characters:** Focusing solely on the protagonist's narrative may result in underdeveloped supporting characters. This can lead to a lack of depth and complexity in the overall story, potentially reducing its impact.

4. **Overemphasis on Internal Monologues:** While internal monologues can provide insights into the protagonist's thoughts and emotions, excessive reliance on this technique may lead to a lack of action and slow down the pacing of the narrative.

5. **Unrealistic Transformation:** If the protagonist's growth and transformation feel unrealistic or poorly justified, it can strain the reader's credibility and engagement. A lack of believability in the transformation may undermine the overall impact of the narrative.

Conclusion

1. creating a meaningful life is a journey of self-discovery, connection, contribution, and personal growth. By identifying our values, pursuing passions, cultivating relationships, serving others, and embracing the present moment, we can craft a life that is truly meaningful to us. It is a continuous process that requires conscious effort and reflection, but the rewards are immeasurable. So let us embark on this journey with an open heart and a willingness to explore the depths of our own existence, as we strive to create a life that is rich, purposeful, and meaningful.

2. The four roles we play in life—the victim, the villain, the protagonist, and the guide—shape our understanding of ourselves and our interactions with the world. Each role presents unique challenges and opportunities for growth. By embracing these roles consciously and with awareness, we can cultivate empathy, resilience, and personal development. Recognizing the victim within us helps us empathize with others and extend compassion. Acknowledging the villain within us fosters self-awareness, growth, and forgiveness. Embracing the protagonist's role empowers us to take charge of our lives and create meaningful experiences. Assuming the guide role allows us to contribute positively to the lives of others and create a ripple effect of inspiration and transformation. Ultimately, by understanding and embodying these roles, we embark on a journey of self-discovery, personal fulfillment, and collective well-being.

3. In literature and storytelling, the embrace of autonomy by protagonists serves as a powerful and resonant theme. Through their transformative journeys, these characters demonstrate the importance of breaking free from societal constraints, empowering oneself, challenging oppressive systems, and overcoming internal struggles. The triumph of the protagonist who embraces their autonomy offers readers a compelling narrative of personal growth, resilience, and the enduring spirit of individuality. It serves as a reminder that each of us can forge our path and shape our destiny, ultimately contributing to a more inclusive and liberated society.

4. The decision of a protagonist to live a meaningful life is a transformative journey that encompasses various dimensions. Through awakening, self-discovery, and the alignment of actions with values, the protagonist embarks on a quest to find purpose. The cultivation of meaningful relationships and the impact on the world further enrich the protagonist's journey. Although challenges may arise, the protagonist's resilience and determination drive them forward. Ultimately, the protagonist reaches a state of transcendence, experiencing a profound sense of fulfillment and leaving a lasting legacy. The protagonist's decision to live a meaningful life serves as an inspiration to all, reminding us of the transformative power of purpose in our own lives.

5. Goals serve as powerful motivational forces that drive protagonists toward their desired outcomes. By providing a sense of purpose, direction, and fulfillment, goals ignite the motivation within protagonists, propelling them through transformative journeys. As we explore the intricate dynamics between goals and protagonists, we unravel the depth and complexity of their character development. Through literature and cinema, we witness the profound impact that goals have in shaping narratives and inspiring audiences. Ultimately, the pursuit of goals unveils the true essence of protagonists, showcasing their resilience, growth, and unwavering determination to achieve their dreams.

6. A morning routine serves as a compass, guiding and directing our personal stories. By consciously designing a routine that encompasses reflection, mindfulness, physical activity, nourishment, and goal-setting, we can shape our narratives with intention and purpose. Through experimentation, adaptation, and a commitment to consistent practice, we can cultivate a morning routine that optimizes our well-being, fuels our productivity, and aligns our actions with our aspirations. Embracing the power of a morning routine empowers us to become the authors of our own stories, taking charge of our lives and creating narratives that are meaningful, fulfilling, and purpose-driven.

7. Crafting a strategy for life empowers individuals to lead intentional, purpose-driven lives. By reflecting on personal values, setting goals, developing skills, managing time effectively, building a support network, and embracing adaptability, individuals can create a roadmap tailored to their aspirations and navigate life's challenges with resilience. Regular evaluation and revision ensure that the strategy remains relevant and aligned with changing circumstances. With a well-crafted life strategy in place, individuals can unlock their full potential and live a life of fulfillment and success.

8. Even before life's end, the act of crafting a eulogy allows individuals to step into the role of the protagonist and reflect on their life's journey. This profound exercise of introspection and self-discovery enables individuals to celebrate their accomplishments, evaluate their impact on others, and contemplate their legacy and purpose. By embracing the transformative power of eulogies, individuals can apply the lessons learned and the insights gained to live a more intentional and meaningful life, making the most of each moment and leaving a lasting impact on the world.

9. A strong eulogy serves as a powerful tool for giving a story momentum, casting the honoree as the protagonist of the narrative. By setting the stage, celebrating individuality, sharing meaningful anecdotes, acknowledging challenges, recognizing relationships, reflecting on impact, and celebrating legacy, the eulogy gains depth, resonance, and forward-moving energy. It becomes a testament to the honoree's life, inspiring others to embrace their own stories with fervor and purpose. As we craft eulogies with care and intention, may we honor the lives of those who have touched us and ensure their stories continue to propel us forward as protagonists in our journeys.

10. Drafting a eulogy as a protagonist allows us to view a person's life as a narrative, celebrating their triumphs, growth, and impact. By exploring their journey through this lens, we can honor and remember them in a unique and meaningful way. Crafting a eulogy from the viewpoint of the protagonist encourages us to reflect on our own lives, inspiring us to embrace our heroic journeys and leave a lasting legacy.

11. The protagonist's medium- and long-term visions revolve around personal growth, making a positive impact on society, pursuing their passions, and fostering meaningful connections. By investing in their development, contributing to causes they care about, aligning their career with their values, and cultivating strong relationships, the

protagonist aims to lead a fulfilling and purposeful life while leaving a positive mark on the world.

12. The completion of tasks by a protagonist serves as a transformative and pivotal element in storytelling. Through these challenges, the hero or heroine undergoes personal growth, acquires new skills, and ultimately fulfills their destiny. The hero's journey, symbolized by task completion, inspires readers, viewers, and players to reflect on their own lives, encouraging resilience, determination, and the pursuit of purpose. By exploring the significance of task completion in narrative arcs, we gain insights into the human condition, the power of perseverance, and the potential for personal and societal transformation.

13 It's important to note that the daily agenda can vary depending on the specific location, culture, and objectives of the missionary work. Adaptations and adjustments may be necessary to accommodate specific circumstances and requirements.

14. The role of protagonists in shaping narratives and inspiring change cannot be overstated. Through their captivating stories, conveyance of themes, embodiment of archetypal qualities, and catalyzation of personal and societal transformations, protagonists leave a lasting impact on audiences. They serve as guides, mentors, and sources of inspiration, encouraging individuals to reflect on their own lives, embrace growth, and contribute to positive change in the world. As we continue to explore the diverse landscape of storytelling, the crucial job of protagonists remains steadfast in captivating our hearts, challenging our minds, and inspiring us to create a better future.

15. The protagonist's narrative is a captivating element that forms the backbone of storytelling. It allows readers to embark on a journey alongside the protagonist, experiencing their triumphs, tribulations, and personal growth. Through the protagonist's narrative, authors can engage readers emotionally, present complex themes, and challenge societal norms. Whether through first-person or third-person perspectives, the narrative perspective shapes the reader's connection with the protagonist. The protagonist's journey unfolds through challenges, self-discovery, and transformation, leaving an indelible impact on the reader's mind. By exploring various genres and analyzing renowned literary works, we have unraveled the profound significance of the protagonist's narrative in the realm of storytelling. As readers, we are fortunate to be able to immerse ourselves in these narratives, gaining insights into the human condition and the potential for personal growth and change.

Afterword

As I reflect upon the journey we have taken together throughout the pages of The Protagonists' Mission, I am filled with a sense of profound gratitude and awe. It is a testament to the power of storytelling and the human imagination, reminding us of the boundless potential that lies within each of us.

In this tale, we witnessed the transformative power of unity, resilience, and the unwavering pursuit of truth. The protagonists, once ordinary individuals thrust into extraordinary circumstances, emerged as beacons of hope and catalysts for change. Their mission, seemingly insurmountable at times, served as a metaphor for the challenges we all face in our own lives.

Through the trials and tribulations they encountered, the protagonists discovered newfound strengths and overcame their deepest fears. They reminded us that within every individual lies the capacity for greatness, waiting to be awakened by the call to action and the refusal to accept the status quo.

The exploration of the hidden world in The Protagonists' Mission revealed not only the dark underbelly of society but also the nuanced shades of grey that exist within the human condition. It forced us to question our own beliefs, confront our own biases, and reevaluate the systems that govern our lives.

As the layers of secrecy were peeled away, we were confronted with uncomfortable truths and forced to confront the consequences of our actions. The book challenged us to examine our roles in perpetuating systems of oppression and offered a glimmer of hope that change is possible if we dare to face our shadows.

The relationships forged within the narrative were a testament to the power of human connection. From the unbreakable bond between the protagonists to the alliances formed with unexpected allies, we witnessed the strength that can be derived from unity and empathy. It is a reminder that we are not alone in our struggles and that the support of others can make all the difference in the pursuit of our missions.

Throughout the story, the protagonists face numerous obstacles that test their resolve and push them to their limits. These challenges served as opportunities for growth, as they were forced to confront their weaknesses, face their deepest fears, and rise above the adversities that threatened to consume them.

But it was not just the physical battles that defined their journey. The internal struggles, the moments of doubt and introspection, were equally significant. It was in these moments of vulnerability that the protagonists truly found themselves, discovering the strength to carry on and the resilience to face whatever lay ahead.

The Protagonists' Mission is not simply a work of fiction; it is a mirror held up to society, reflecting the complexities of our world. It invites us to examine the systems that govern our lives, question the narratives we have been fed, and challenge the status quo. It is a reminder that change starts with each one of us and that our actions, however small, can have ripple effects that extend far beyond ourselves.

As we close the final chapter of this book, let us carry with us the lessons learned from the protagonists' mission. Let us remember that within us lies the potential to be agents of change, to challenge injustice, and to create a world that is more just, equitable, and compassionate.

The Protagonists' Mission serves as a reminder that stories have the power to inspire, ignite our imaginations, and spark conversations that can shape the world we live in. I hope that this story catalyzes dialogue, encouraging readers to question the narratives they encounter and empowering them to create their narrative of change.

In conclusion, I would like to express my deepest gratitude to every reader who has embarked on this journey with me. Your support, and your willingness to engage with these characters and their struggles, are what breathes life into this story. May The

Protagonists' Mission continue to inspire and empower, reminding us all that our missions, however daunting, are worth pursuing.

With heartfelt appreciation,

[Dr. Amelia Hartley. PhD.